THE
REFERENCE
SHELF

RELIGIOUS CULTS

IN AMERICA

Edited by ROBERT EMMET LONG

THE REFERENCE SHELF

Volume 66 Number 4

94-232

THE H. W. WILSON COMPANY

New York   1994

THE REFERENCE SHELF

The books in this series contain reprints of articles, excerpts from books, and addresses on current issues and social trends in the United States and other countries. There are six separately bound numbers in each volume, all of which are generally published in the same calendar year. One number is a collection of recent speeches; each of the others is devoted to a single subject and gives background information and discussion from various points of view, concluding with a comprehensive bibliography that contains books and pamphlets and abstracts of additional articles on the subject. Books in the series may be purchased individually or on subscription.

Library of Congress Cataloging-in-Publication Data

Religious cults in America / edited by Robert Emmet Long.
     p. cm. — (The Reference shelf ; v. 66, no. 4)
    Includes bibliographical references.
    ISBN 0-8242-0855-2
    1. Cults—United States. 2. Branch Davidians. 3. Waco Branch Davidian Disaster, Tex., 1993. I. Long, Robert Emmet. II. Series.
BL2525.R469 1994
291.9'0973—dc20   94-16329
                                             CIP

Cover: Rainbow Family members share prayers for peace.

Photo: AP/Wide World Photos

Printed in the United States of America

CONTENTS

IV. CULTS AND CONTROVERSY

V. CULTS AND THE MEDIA

PREFACE

One of the most sensational occurrences of 1993 was the FBI raid on the Branch Davidian compound, and the ensuing fire that killed cult leader David Koresh and scores of his followers, including dozens of children. This episode was the final installment of a drama that began with the Bureau of Alcohol Tobacco and Firearm's (ATF) initial assault on the compound. An assault that resulted in fatalities on both sides. Ironically, both Koresh and the government displayed a fascination for guns. Koresh was a holder of extreme views, believing that he alone possessed the word of God, and that he must arm his compound for the day it would be under attack by external, ungodly forces. Koresh's violent, final vision held a death wish that would be fulfilled in the news greedy glare of the media. This, coupled with federal agents who were both heavy-handed and determined to display their military prowess, acted as the seed for the final conflagration.

This Reference Shelf volume contains articles on the Branch Davidian tragedy and on American cults in general. In section one, the opening article discusses the mass suicide of 900 members of the People's Temple in Guyana. The next article depicts the last days of Koresh's Ranch Apocalypse. David Koresh is described as a misfit who, like Jim Jones before him, gained absolute sovereignty over his followers. Other articles in section one, two and three debate whether the outcome of the standoff would have been different if the government had been more tactful and patient. Also considered are the children who left the compound before the April showdown and will continue to live with the scars of their Branch Davidian experience. In these first three sections a debate arises—the danger of cults headed by leaders who have acquired power and lost their sense of reality versus the first amendment's protection of the "free exercise" of religion.

Sections four and five of this compilation move beyond the Branch Davidian debate and examine the array of marginal or alternative religions that exist in America today. J. Gordon Melton's brief guide provides a useful and ample introduction to these American cults. This guide is complemented by other pieces that focus upon the controversy surrounding non-mainstream religions. Section four is concerned with an examination of specific "churches." They include Satanism, Santeria, the Church of

Scientology, and the latest global maneuvers of the Unification Church's Sun Myung Moon.

The editor is indebted to the authors and publishers who have granted permission to reprint the materials contained in this collection. Special thanks are due to Joyce Cook and the Fulton, N.Y. Public Library staff, and to the staff of the Penfield Library at the State University of New York, Oswego.

ROBERT EMMET LONG

January 1994

I. DAVID KORESH AND THE TRAGEDY AT WACO

EDITOR'S INTRODUCTION

When the FBI moved against the Branch Davidian compound outside Waco in April 1993, one had an eerie sense of history repeating itself. There was an unmistakable resemblance between Jim Jones and David Koresh—both charismatic leaders who stood at the absolute center of religious cults, and preferred death for themselves and their followers rather than surrender to the vested authorities of the state. The final hour of Jones's People's Temple and Koresh's Branch Davidians was grisly and spectacular receiving intense media coverage. The death toll in the South American jungle near Georgetown, Guyana was over 900, in Texas about 90. In both cases, many innocent children were among the casualties.

In the opening article in Section One, Keith Harrary in *Psychology Today* discusses the final days of Jim Jones and his People's Temple. According to survivors' accounts, Jones's original ideals had been corrupted; his leadership in the commune had been marked by fraudulent practices like mind control, and indulgence in sexual perversions. His career illustrates the vulnerability of cultic groups, in which a single individual holds total power. The following piece by Ivan Solotaroff in *Esquire* is an eyewitness account of the conflagration at David Koresh's appropriately named Ranch Apocalypse. Solotaroff comments on Koresh's background as a ninth-grade dropout and misfit who had fanatical fixations with heavy metal rock music and apocalyptic religion. He explores Koresh's involvement with Branch Davidian prophetess Lois Roden and her son George, once Koresh's rival for control of the Branch Davidians and now confined to a mental institution. This is a brilliantly written piece that gives a strong impression of Koresh's world.

Gordon Witkin's article, in *U.S. News & World Report*, comments on Koresh's stockpiling of weapons, including 45 machine guns, 1.8 million rounds of ammunition, two .50-caliber Barrett rifles capable of hitting targets more than a mile away, and over three dozen assault-style rifles. These weapons were acquired, over a two-year period, at gun shows and by mail order. Although machine guns were illegal, the Branch Davidians contrived to assemble them from semi-automatic weapons and "replacement parts" for machine guns. Koresh's obsession with weaponry ultimately proved his undoing. A box being delivered by a UPS employee broke open to reveal a cargo of 50 grenades, and spurred an F.B.I. investigation of the Branch Davidians. The following article by James Popkin and Jeannye Thornton, also in *U.S. News & World Report,* discusses the ATF's blundering initial assault on the compound, as well as the phenomenon of cults—like the Aryan Nation in Idaho and the Church Universal and Triumphant in Montana—that also amass stores of weapons. The concluding article, "Tripped Up by Lies," by Howard Chua-Eoan, reports on the 220-page critique of the ATF, recently issued by the Treasury Department. Because of its poorly planned siege on the compound and its subsequent lies and obfuscation, the ATF's entire top management has been fired.

THE TRUTH ABOUT JONESTOWN[1]

The old Peoples Temple building collapsed in the last big San Francisco earthquake, leaving behind nothing but an empty plot of land to mark its passing. I'd avoided the place for nearly 10 years—it always struck me as a dark reminder of the raw vulnerability of the human mind and the superficial nature of civilized behavior. In ways that I never expected when I first decided to investigate the Jonestown holocaust, the crimes that took place within that building and within the cult itself have become a part of my personal memory. If Jim Jones has finally become a metaphor, a symbol of power-hungry insanity—if not a term for insanity itself—for me he will always remain much too human.

Suicide is usually an act of lonely desperation, carried out in isolation or near isolation by those who see death as an acceptable alternative to the burdens of continued existence. It can also be

[1]Article by Keith Harrary, president and research director of the Institute for Advanced Psychology, San Francisco. From *Psychology Today* 25:62–69+ Mr '92. Copyright © 1992 by Sussex Publishers, Inc. Reprinted with permission of Psychology Today magazine.

an act of self-preservation among those who prefer a dignified death to the ravages of illness or some perceived humiliation. It is even, occasionally, a political statement. But it is rarely, if ever, a social event. The reported collective self-extermination of 912 individuals (913 when Jim Jones was counted among their number) therefore demanded more than an ordinary explanation.

The only information I had about Jim Jones was what I could gather from news accounts of the closing scene at the Jonestown compound. The details were sketchy but deeply disturbing: The decomposing corpses were discovered in the jungle in the stinking aftermath of a suicidal frenzy set around a vat of cyanide-laced Flavor-Aid. Littered among the dead like broken dolls were the bodies of 276 children. A United States congressman and three members of the press entourage traveling with him were ambushed and murdered on an airstrip not far from the scene. It had all been done in the name of a formerly lesser-known cult called the Peoples Temple.

The group was started years before with the avowed vision of abolishing racism. Although it was headquartered in San Francisco, its members sought to found their own Utopia in a nondescript plot of South American jungle near Georgetown, Guyana. The commune they created was named in honor of the cult's founder and religious leader, a charismatic figure in dark glasses named the Reverend Jim Jones.

While the news media treated the Jonestown holocaust like a fluke of nature, it seemed to me a unique opportunity to learn something crucial about the fundamental weakness of the human mind. In addition to my formal education in psychology, I had recently spent four years as a suicide-prevention counselor and had helped train dozens of other counselors working in the field. But even with that experience, the slaughter that took place in Jonestown seemed incomprehensible.

No casual observer could adequately explain what was happening in the minds of the Peoples Temple members when they allowed Jones to assume ultimate power over their lives. The question of how *one* person—nonetheless an entire group—could be motivated to give away such power was, however, the most critical one to ask. Not only was it essential to answer that question in order to explain what became of the Peoples Temple; it was equally crucial to answer it in order to prevent a similar tragedy from happening again in the future.

Had the massacre succeeded in killing all the witnesses to

what occurred inside the confines of Jonestown, it would have been impossible to get a believable answer. But there were a number of survivors: An old woman sleeping in a hut slipped the minds of her fellow members who were preoccupied with dying at the time; a nine-year-old girl survived having her throat cut by a member who then committed suicide; a young man worked his way to the edge of the compound and fled into the jungle. The only other eyewitness escaped when he was sent to get a stethoscope so the bodies could be checked to make certain they were dead.

Other survivors included a man wounded by gunfire at the airstrip who managed to escape by scrambling into the bush; the official Peoples Temple basketball team (including Jones's son), which was visiting Georgetown during the holocaust; a number of members stationed at the San Francisco headquarters; and a small group of defectors and relatives of those who had remained in the cult. The last was gathered at a place called the Human Freedom Center in Berkeley—a halfway house for cult defectors founded by Jeannie and Al Mills, two Peoples Temple expatriates.

Since most of the survivors lived in and around San Francisco, it was clear that in order to get to know any of them, I would have to be willing to go where the moment took me. I resigned from my position in the psychiatry department of a New York medical center, shipped most of what I owned to a storage facility, and moved to California. Shortly after arriving, I learned that the center was looking for a director of counseling. It was exactly the position I wanted.

It is impossible to look back on my first encounter with Jeannie and Al [Mills] without coloring the memory with the knowledge that both of them were murdered almost exactly one year later. We met in the same room where they had once helped Congressman Leo Ryan plan his ill-fated expedition to Jonestown, which was mounted to give him and the press a close-up look at the cult and to offer any constituents who wanted safe passage an opportunity to return to San Francisco. They had hoped the visit would precipitate the demise of the Peoples Temple, but instead of allowing his game to be raided, Jones had Ryan killed and passed out the poison. The Millses never imagined the scenic route to hell they were paving with their good intentions: Had they not convinced the congressman to go to Guyana, the massacre would most likely never have happened.

In the years that have passed since the Millses' assassination, I have never again been able to take a death threat lightly.

The pair had been members of the Planning Commission—the elite inner circle of the Peoples Temple. They had been with Jim Jones since the early days of the cult and had raised hundreds of thousands of dollars for his cause. But Jeannie wanted a bigger role in running the group than Jones was prepared to give her. His refusal to allow her to manage the affairs of the temple created a bitter falling-out between them. She and Al quit after spending six years in the cult, fearing for their lives because Jones always threatened that anyone who left would be murdered by his "angels"—a euphemism for his personal squad of thugs.

Jones had forced them to prove their loyalty by signing blank pieces of paper, blank power-of-attorney forms, and false confessions that they had molested their children, conspired to overthrow the U.S. government, and committed other crimes while members of the cult. (It was the sort of thing Jones did to control people, like the time he tricked a member into putting her fingerprints on a gun and told her he would have someone killed with it and frame her for the murder if she ever left the group.)

There was a deliberate malevolence about the way Jones treated the members of his cult that went beyond mere perversion. It was all about forcing members to experience themselves as vulgar and despicable people who could never return to a normal life outside of the group. It was about destroying any personal relationships that might come ahead of the relationship each individual member had with him. It was about terrorizing children and turning them against their parents. It was about seeing Jim Jones as an omnipotent figure who could snuff out members' lives on a whim as easily as he had already snuffed out their self-respect. In short, it was about mind control. And, after all that, it was not incidentally about Jones's own sick fantasies and sexual perversions.

Both men and women were routinely beaten, coerced into having sex with Jones in private and with other people in public. Husbands and wives were forbidden to have sex with each other, but were forced to join other members in watching their spouses being sexually humiliated and abused. In order to prove that he wasn't a racist, a white man was coerced into having oral sex in front of a gathering of members with a black woman who was having her period. Another man was made to remove all his clothes, bend over and spread his legs before the congregation while being examined for signs of venereal disease. A woman had to strip in front of the group so that Jones could poke fun at her overweight body before telling her to submerge herself in a pool of ice-cold water. Another woman was made to squat in front of 100 members and defecate into a fruit can. Children were tortured with electric shocks, viciously beaten, punished by being kept in the bottom of a jungle well, forced to have hot peppers stuffed up their rectums, and made to eat their own vomit.

Dozens of suicide drills—or "white nights" as Jim Jones called them—were rehearsed in San Francisco and in the jungle in a prelude to the final curtain he said might fall at any moment. Members were given wine to drink, then told it had been poisoned to test their loyalty and get them used to the idea that they might all be asked to take their lives as a sign of their faith. Their deaths, Jones tried to convince them, would be honored by the world as a symbolic protest against the evils of mankind—a collective self-immolation. (This would also serve to eliminate anyone who might reveal the dirty secrets of life with the Peoples Temple.) The faithful would be "transformed," Jones claimed, and live with him forever on another planet.

The abuses had been going on for years, which made it seem all the more unbelievable. Those who underestimated the fragility of the human mind could not comprehend how anyone in California could remain a member, let alone follow Jim Jones into the jungle. Yet those who believed in him could not consider any alternatives that were not among the choices he provided. Even those who might have been capable of imagining themselves getting free of the cult knew about the stated policy of murdering defectors. And since any loved ones who were left behind would suffer retribution, few dared escape while family members remained in Jonestown. The practical effect of that double bind was a twilight-zone reality in which people pretended to be enjoying a Utopian existence while living in constant fear for their lives.

The Human Freedom Center was a beaten-up, two-story wood-and-stucco building that had once been used as a private rest home. Its long rows of odd-size rooms filled with broken-down furniture could have served as a backdrop for a 1950s horror movie set in a sanitarium. Although most of the Peoples Temple survivors who might have taken refuge there were suddenly dead, the events in Jonestown instantly made many other organizations seem potentially as dangerous. Jeannie and Al decided to open the center to defectors from all sorts of cult groups, from the Unification Church to the Hare Krishnas. I had already decided that—whatever the pay—if they offered me the director of counseling position, I was going to take it.

Al Mills gripped my hand like an old war buddy the first time we met. His square chin and warm smile all but obliterated the other features on his face. He had marched with Martin Luther King and once believed that the Peoples Temple would fulfill his dream of integration and racial equality. (That belief was trampled when he realized that Jones rarely allowed blacks to assume positions of authority within the temple.)

My first discussion with Jeannie was less like a job interview than a confrontation. She looked straight at me and said that a Peoples Temple hit squad might burst in and kill us at any moment. Jim Jones, she said, had sworn in the midst of the holocaust that she and Al and everyone associated with them would eventually pay with their lives for betraying the cult and sending Ryan to Guyana. The possibility lent a certain sense of immediacy to our interaction.

My exact response seemed less important than the fact that I didn't make an excuse to leave the building immediately and that I had already demonstrated my commitment to understanding the cult mentality by dropping everything and moving to California. By the end of the meeting, Jeannie offered me a token salary for a job that would often require more than 12 hours a day and frequently seven days a week.

Most of the center's clients were people seeking help in extricating family members from various cults, or ex-cult members who were starting to put their own lives back together. Additionally, a couple of former Peoples Temple members lived on the premises, and others came in periodically to talk about their present feelings and past experiences.

The first thing that struck me when I met the clients and got to know them was that, although the specific details of their belief systems and activities varied considerably, those who became involved in cults had a frightening underlying commonality. They described their experiences as finding an unexpected sense of purpose, as though they were becoming a part of something extraordinarily significant that seemed to carry them beyond their feelings of isolation and toward an expanded sense of reality and the meaning of life. Nobody asked if they would be willing to commit suicide the first time they attended a meeting. Nor did anyone mention that the feeling of expansiveness they were enjoying would later be used to turn them against each other.

Instead they were told about the remarkable Reverend Jones, a self-professed social visionary and prophet who apparently could heal the sick and predict the future. Jim Jones did everything within his power to perpetuate that myth: fraudulent psychic-healing demonstrations using rotting animal organs as phony tumors; searching through members' garbage for information to reveal in fake psychic readings; drugging his followers to make it appear as though he were actually raising the dead. Even Jeannie Mills, who later told me she knowingly assisted Jones in his faked demonstrations, said she did so because she believed she was helping him conserve his real supernatural powers for more important matters.

Critical levels of sleep deprivation can masquerade as noble dedication. A total lack of adequate nutrition can seem acceptable when presented as a reasonable sacrifice for a worthy cause. Combining the two for a prolonged length of time will inevitably break down the ability to make rational judgments and weaken the psychological resistance of anyone. So can the not-infrequent practice of putting drugs in the members' food. The old self, the one that previously felt lonely and lacking in a sense of purpose, is gradually overcome by a new sense of self inextricably linked with the feeling of expansiveness associated with originally joining the cult and becoming intrigued with its leader.

Belonging to the group gradually becomes more important than anything else. When applied in various combinations, fear of being rejected, of doing or saying something wrong that will blow the whole illusion wide open; being punished and degraded, subjected to physical threats, unprovoked violence, and sexual abuse; fear of never amounting to anything; and the fear of returning to an old self associated almost exclusively with feelings of loneliness and a lack of meaning will confuse almost anyone. Patricia Hearst knows all about it. So did all the members of the Peoples Temple.

Once thrown off balance (in the exclusive company of other people who already believe it) and being shown evidence that supports the conclusion, it is not difficult to become convinced that you have actually met the Living God. In the glazed and pallid stupor associated with achieving that confused and dangerous state of mind, almost any conceivable act of self-sacrifice, self-degradation, and cruelty can become possible.

The truth of that realization was brought home to me by one survivor who, finding himself surrounded by rifles, was told he could take the poison quietly or they would stick it in his veins or blow his brains out. He didn't resist. Instead, he raised his cup and toasted those dying around him without drinking. "We'll see each other in the transformation," he said. Then he walked around the compound shaking hands until he'd worked his way to the edge of the jungle, where he ran and hid until he felt certain it had to be over.

"Why did you follow Jim Jones?" I asked him.

"Because I believed he was God," he answered. "We all believed he was God."

A number of Peoples Temple survivors told me they viewed Jones in the same way—not as God metaphorically, but as God *literally*. They would have done anything he asked of them, they said. Or almost anything.

The fact that some members held guns on the others and handled the syringes meant that what occurred in Jonestown was not only a mass suicide but also a mass murder. According to the witnesses, more than one member was physically restrained while being poisoned. A little girl kept spitting out the poison until they held her mouth closed and forced her to swallow it—276 children do not calmly kill themselves just because someone who claims to be God tells them to. A woman was found with nearly every joint in her body yanked apart from trying to pull away from the people who were holding her down and poisoning her. All 912 Peoples Temple members did not die easily.

Yet even if all the victims did not take their own lives willingly, enough of them probably did so that we cannot deny the force of their conviction. Only a small contingent of Peoples Temple members asked to return with Leo Ryan to San Francisco. The rest chose to stay behind. Jim Jones may have had less to fear from Jeannie and Al Mills than he believed.

It should also be remembered that Jones never took the poison he gave to his followers but was shot by someone else during the final death scene in Jonestown. He created a false reality around himself in which the denial of his own mortality must have made his own demise seem inconceivable. The fact that he had millions of dollars in foreign bank accounts and had often alluded to starting over elsewhere led Jeannie to speculate that he planned to escape the holocaust but was murdered by one of his guards or mistresses.

It is difficult to imagine what incomprehensible sense of insecurity must have led Jim Jones to feel that he had to convince himself and other people that he was God incarnate. It was not a delusion that he ever suffered well. Some of those who knew him personally described him to me at various times as a mere voyeur, a master con artist, a sociopath, and a demon. Al Mills once said that any private interaction between Jones and another person always felt like a "conspiracy of two." For my own part, I resist any description of the man that might make any of us feel too secure in the notion that he was one of a kind and the likes of him will never come again.

After Jeannie and Al were murdered, I went back alone for a final look inside the Peoples Temple building where Jeannie once gave me a private tour. All that remained of that particular nightmare setting was a dusty maze of dimly lit corridors, hollow rooms, and twisting stairways. The daylight seemed reluctant to come in through the windows, as though it entered more out of a sense of obligation than any real desire to be there. It was impossible to walk through the place without feeling as though somebody were coming up behind me—nearly everything about it seemed haunted.

"This may not be the best idea in the world," I remembered Jeannie saying when she took me there. "There may be some people hanging around here who want to kill me." It may have been guilt that led her to say that, or paranoia, or the realistic conclusion that the relatives and friends of many of the victims must have held her at least partly responsible for what happened. The Jonestown holocaust might have been inevitable or it might have been avoided; but by turning up the pressure on Jones in the way that they did, Jeannie and Al inextricably became accessories to the disaster.

Under the circumstances, I suggested that getting the hell out of there might be the best approach. "Life is short, Keith," Jeannie told me. She showed me where Jones's personal armed guards had once been posted, before taking me to lunch at a hamburger stand where she used to hang out in the heyday of the temple.

In many ways, Jeannie was a social relic of the best and worst aspects of a way of life that died in the jungle with Jim Jones. She said and did things designed for their disarming effect, to crawl around under your skin and keep you off guard. She was an expert at making you feel that you were a part of something important, dangerous, and utterly surrealistic—and she may have been right. It did not surprise me to learn that she was monitoring my personal telephone conversations at the Human

Freedom Center from a line she had installed at her home up the street. It was exactly the way things were done in the Peoples Temple.

Al Mills was found on the bedroom floor of the cottage that he and Jeannie shared, with a single bullet in the head. He may have been going for the gun he once told me that he kept there. Jeannie was found behind the kicked-in door of the adjoining bathroom, also shot once in the head. It looked as though she had tried to escape from her murderer by running into a room that had no exit. Their daughter, Daphene—who may or may not have just happened to be there—was found lying on the bed above Al, with a bullet in her head and three or four other bullets in the mattress surrounding her. A neighbor had reportedly heard two male voices outside, and one of them saying, "You're not gonna pin it on me," before the three bodies were found. The victims were reportedly shot with .22-caliber bullets, coincidentally the alleged preferred choice of professional assassins. Jeannie and Al's young son, Eddie, was found listening to a stereo with headphones in the other room of the tiny cottage when the bodies were discovered. He told the police that he didn't hear anything at all while both his parents and his sister were being killed. He had grown up in the Peoples Temple. The case is still open.

For my own part, I believe that Jeannie and Al were victims of their fatalistic vision of reality and that whoever pulled the trigger completed a course of events that was set into motion years before. In their inability to otherwise put to rest their experiences in the cult, they had never really left the Peoples Temple.

For those of us whose lives were directly touched by the massacre, the images of Jonestown have never entered the realm of dispassionate historical memory. They remain a part of the hidden present, providing a point of reference in defining the conditions under which people can be led across the boundary between rational and extremely irrational behavior.

Had more of the children of Jonestown survived, they might have tried to warn us that we have more to fear than the fact that whoever murdered Jeannie and Al is still on the loose and may kill again. A lone fanatic is much less dangerous than the potential that exists within all of us for committing evil ourselves or allowing it to be committed in the name of some supposed good. There is no doubt that there are—*right now*—other cult groups that hold the same potential for deadly violence as did the Peoples Temple.

Jim Jones did not create the human weaknesses that led so many people to follow him; he merely exploited them. Ultimate power is seductive not only to those who achieve it themselves but also to those who give up their own power in order to help others achieve it. It is the ability to answer the unanswerable questions about the meaning of life and death. And it does not matter if those answers make no sense—the belief in them and in the individual who bears them makes any sacrifice in the service of some more eternal purpose seem acceptable.

Most of us don't think of ourselves as the kind of person who could ever possibly become embroiled in a cult like the Peoples Temple. We are not at all correct in that assumption. Given an unfortunate turn of fate that leads to a moment of weakness, or a momentary lapse in judgment that expands into a shift in our perception, nearly any of us could find ourselves taking the cyanide in Jonestown—if not passing out the poison to other people.

People end up joining cults when events lead them to search for a deeper sense of belonging and for something more meaningful in their lives. They do so because they happen to be in the wrong place at the wrong time and are ripe for exploitation. They do so because they find themselves getting caught in the claws of a parasite before they realize what is happening to them.

Those who join cults don't do so with the intention of demeaning themselves or torturing children. They join in the hope of creating a better world, and because they believe in a lie, or a series of lies, in the same way that the rest of us sometimes find ourselves falling in love with the wrong person or allowing ourselves to be manipulated. The only real difference between them and us is the extent to which they are led to carry those same sorts of feelings to extremes.

The spectre of Jonestown has entered the social unconscious, leading to a kind of macabre fascination with Jim Jones and his victims. A Boston company recently sold out its first printing of "Death Cult" cards commemorating the massacre; they depict such images as "Spiking the Kool-Aid." At least for those not directly involved, the unthinkably horrific has become entertaining. We dissociate ourselves as human beings from any sense of connectedness to Jonestown by turning the event into a kind of theater. But it was that same sense of theater upon which Jim Jones depended, as has every cult leader who has ever exploited human weakness. If you have ever slowed down and stared at the results of a highway accident, you are not immune.

THE LAST REVELATION FROM WACO[2]

In the waist-high underbrush, the first hints of Armageddon are the animals. Jackrabbits, armadillos, polecats, field mice, and rats are darting past me on their way out of the thicket as I make my way in. The buzzards come minutes later, heading in the same direction I am, their white wing tips barely visible above the pine trees as they fly against the strong southeast wind toward Mount Carmel. Deeper into the thicket, a hot gust brings the first black smoke and an odor of burning fuel so strong that it masks whatever other smells might be rising from the burning compound.

I'm not supposed to be here. But after fifty-one days of abiding the FBI's two-and-a-half-mile perimeter and absolute control of information, I'm not going to watch the endgame from the press center at "Satellite City," especially now that the FBI has breached the walls of the Davidian sanctum. I follow the tree line until I'm within three quarters of a mile of the conflagration at Mount Carmel and can taste the smoke with every gust.

This is as close as I get. Between me and all that's left of Rancho Apocalypse stands a row of thirty-five to forty agents of the Bureau of Alcohol, Tobacco, and Firearms, bearing M-16's and special-issue 9-mm handguns. It seems wise to head back into the thicket, but before I go, I pause and look over my shoulder, like Lot's wife, at one final image of church and state at war: Highlighted by the scrim of the inferno, an M-1 tank's American flag and Mount Carmel's blue-bordered Star of David flap furiously against each other.

The ground begins to shake with a terrible rumbling as a sleek, blue FBI chopper heads toward Mount Carmel. The chopper is halfway there when the Star of David finally snaps off its pole and sails into the fire. With the flag's disappearance goes seven weeks of waiting out a national obsession that turned on David Koresh's predilection for big guns, rock 'n' roll, and sex with underage girls. That is, if you can believe the media. I've been waiting for the other side of this story, limited thus far to one rambling local radio broadcast by Koresh, warnings of earth-

[2]Article by Ivan Solotaroff. Copyright © 1993 by Ivan Solotaroff. Reprinted with permission of Wylie, Aitken & Stone, Inc. First published in *Esquire* 120: 52–55+ Jl '93.

quakes and comets, a few banners hung from Mount Carmel's watchtower, late-night Morse code, a few holy fools, and the odd Libertarian.

The ground rumbles again as a Chinook, brought in to airlift casualties, clears the eastern edge of the thicket and circles Mount Carmel. Suddenly it's manifest how horribly the battle between two irreconcilable factions—those waiting for Judgment Day and a state that reserves judgment for itself—is being resolved in this combustion.

Directly above me, two Hueys clear the tree line, three armed agents riding shotgun on each. For weeks they've been buzzing the media at Satellite City, causing flashbacks among the Vietnam vets in the working press, forcing us all to now consider with new vehemence a simple question: Why are we in Waco?

When that rumbling first sounded over State Highway 84, just after 9:30 Sunday morning seven weeks before, most people dressing for church just figured it was the Wings of Christ, the fraternal mission that trains local pilots for missionary work in Mexico. Joe Robert, an aircraft-support technician, was loading powder into shells for the Ruger .44 magnum he keeps with his nine other guns in a second fridge in his trailer off the highway. He looked out the kitchen window at the rotary cannon on the black Apache helicopter and knew better. So did Louise, who table-dances at a Waco club with a ring in her clitoris. The vibration of the two Sikorsky Black Hawks, leading the Apache in a southeast pass a mile down 84, made her son's rocking horse on the front lawn move as if some huge man were on it. Vernon, or David Koresh, or whatever he was calling himself now, hadn't been in to see her since the club near Mount Carmel closed because of dancers testing HIV-positive, but she knew the gunships were headed for the Branch Davidians. A lawman in her new club Saturday night had been swearing people to secrecy about a raid next morning, and he did it so well there wasn't anyone there who hadn't been sworn by the time the place closed.

George Baty was milking his cows when the two cattle trucks moved down Farm-to-Market Road 2491 toward Mount Carmel, led by a McClennan County deputy with his blue lights flashing. Behind it was a Ford Bronco and a wagon marked with a TV station's logo. J. D. Lempley, a sixty-five-year-old concrete contractor, was also suspicious when the three helicopters made their second pass over his mesquite woods off Old Mexia Road. He'd been hearing Koresh practicing with his 50 caliber in the pasture behind his land for months, *boump boump boump boump,* and that was just too much advertisement.

Inside Mount Carmel's thirteen buildings, word had also gone out, and the Davidians were in camouflage when the ATF agents bolted out of the cattle trucks to announce their search and arrest warrants. It will probably never be known how the firing started—some say an accidental ATF shot triggered it, others that the report of an ATF multiple-fire concussion grenade was mistaken for automatic fire and returned as such. "Within five minutes," says Greg, a New Orleans ATF agent assigned to the southern buildings, "we'd fired our load and were pinned down. We had control while serving the warrants. After that, it was like lambs to the slaughter."

In the next five weeks, references to these warrants came as frequently and inchoately as Koresh's invocations of the Seven Seals. At daily press briefings, ATF spokesman Dan Conroy, looking as if he had stepped off a 1950s Jesuit campus, deflected all questions about the contradictions and needlessness of the raid with seigneurial assurances that the warrants would clarify everything. Unsealed two days after the fire, they conjured only the same unsubstantiated, ungrammatical preaching to the choir as Koresh's radio broadcast. The image they leave is sad, pathetic, actually: two pariah groups, operating on the edge of the law, both hoping for salvation—the Davidians, to be "the first of the first harvest" at the end of time; the ATF, vestigial revenuers with no clear mandate, from an imminent House budget review. As with the FBI negotiations that would follow, the misunderstanding was willful, a deliberate failure to communicate. When Sue Fatta, a Davidian caught outside Mount Carmel after the ATF raid, read about herself in the *Fort Worth Star-Telegram* two weeks into the siege, it was the first newspaper she'd read in four years. When Bill Clinton drove by Mount Carmel last fall, on a campaign visit to the nearby TU electric plant, the Davidians armed themselves to the teeth, then wondered why the motorcade passed by without attacking. And when Koresh received word of the imminent ATF raid, there was no doubt in his mind who this enemy was: "The Assyrians," he told the Davidians, "are coming."

Pariah leader of a pariah sect that had twice schismed off a pariah religion, Koresh never doubted he was a law unto himself. Regulations concerning firearms, marriage, and compulsory education were not his concern. "See those people?" he asked an Australian correspondent in 1991, pointing rather incredulously to Davidians repairing a roof at Mount Carmel. "*They* think I'm the son of God."

Like Christ's, much of Koresh's early years is lost to obscurity and wanderings. He was an aloof kid, preyed on and sodomized by older boys, and prone to excessive masturbation. His grandmother, Jean Holub, a Seventh-day Adventist, was his great solace: She took him to Saturday church services when he was six, and it had a huge impact. Sitting vigil in her 4×4 at the last checkpoint to Mount Carmel, she tells me how "Vern immediately felt such a peace in the church." He loved foreboding passages of scripture, which, she said, "he just kind of inhaled."

Dyslexic, he spent elementary school in the special-education room and dropped out of Garland High School in the ninth grade, a detail that FBI special agent Bob Ricks made reference to at press briefings but which did not shame Koresh: "Nowhere is it written in the gospel," he taught, "that Christ ever attended these schools." He worked at gas stations and garages, then as a drywaller and landscaper, learned guitar, wrote songs, and haunted clubs in the Dallas area. In 1977 he moved from Garland to Tyler, an oppressive, God-fearing city of seventy thousand in east Texas, and he didn't do well there. Tyler is not a rock 'n' roll town, and the small congregation of the Seventh-day Adventist church, located in a warren of minor Baptist churches on the southern loop off the state highway, "disfellowshiped" Koresh two years later for fighting for power. He headed out to Los Angeles several times, trying to make it at clubs on the Strip and with Adventist congregations, but wound up back in Tyler each time. He got married and divorced on one trip, and later claimed to have become a Satan worshiper and heavy-metal fanatic on another. After the last trip he said he had had a mystical conversion in a Tyler graveyard.

In 1980 his mother became fascinated with the teachings of a sixty-one-year-old prophetess named Lois Roden, the most recent leader of the Branch Davidians. Vernon drove up to Mount Carmel the following spring for a Feast of New Moon service and luncheon and listened to Lois's sermon on the Holy Spirit, which she identified as feminine, perhaps herself. By 1982 he was her constant companion and chauffeur. By 1983 he was answering the phone in her bedroom at 2:00 A.M. and had assumed the role of prophet, a latter-day David, heir to Mount Carmel's "Throne of David," and as the Lamb of God, scheduled to marry Lois, the Bride of Christ.

Instead, he married two underage Davidian girls and inaugurated a concubine system called the House of David, predicated on a complicated contextualization of passages from Psalms, Daniel, and Revelation. Sometimes it was a lot simpler: "Vernon," a seventeen-year-old Australian girl who spent time at Mount Carmel told her parents, "wants me to be his teddy bear tonight."

Such practices prompted a power struggle with Lois's forty-five-year-old son, George, who felt *he* was heir to the throne. After failing to sway the congregation that Koresh was in fact the Mahershlalasbaz Prophet, who "failed the grand test of the kings of Zion to not multiply wives," George brought rape charges against Koresh, naming his mother an "involuntary plaintiff," and brought the first guns to Mount Carmel: an Uzi semiautomatic and a .357 that couldn't shoot straight. He finally won legal title to the property, booted Koresh off, and began preaching sermons that ended "In the name of George Roden, amen." Lois was conflicted: "There are so many contenders for the Throne of David," she wrote. "Seems anyone can become a prophet these days."

In April 1984 Koresh was wandering again, now with a following of nine families. He bought twenty acres of wooded land near Palestine, Texas. There was one primitive building of pine logs; the families lived in abandoned school buses and shacks with no running water or electricity. After a year "in the wilderness," as he later called it, he took off for Australia, California, Hawaii, Israel, and England, where he found some two dozen West Indian converts.

Though he was anything but charismatic when he first wandered into Mount Carmel, by 1988, when he managed to wrest the property from George Roden, he seemed to have gotten the gift: "My tongue," he would tell the flock, quoting Scripture, "is a ready writer." He sinned and contradicted himself openly, but always with disparate chapter-and-verse citations to support himself. Interpreting these passages, he would stare the congregation down with a look of such threat and personal suffering that the dimples of his beatific smile a moment later seemed nothing less than absolution. His key word, borrowed from songwriting, was *harmonizing*. "No one," says Oliver Gyarfas, a twenty-one-year-old Australian who followed his father to Mount Carmel, "ever put such beautiful phrases together out of Scripture."

Koresh also had a remarkable ability to be known to people as they knew themselves. He professed a divine calling to a good many non-Davidians but to no one who would have found it strange. "Saying God talks to you is not unusual," says Joe Robert, whose son went to Axtell High School with Davidian kids. "Down here, that's like saying the Avon lady called." When an Australian TV reporter took Koresh to dinner at the Waco Hilton, a waiter overhearing the interview finally just had to break in: "Thank you, Vernon," he said. "Praise God, you saved my life."

To farmers and tradesmen in the Waco area, Koresh was precise, peaceable, and well versed in the details of their trade. (One farmer told me, "If you're gonna write somethin' bad about David, I don't want to talk to you.") Koresh could talk Sheetrock, livestock maintenance, field rotation, and turbos with anyone and had, like Elvis, a dealership for Go-Karts and Jet Skis. "It can get dull out here," he explained. "People gotta have something to do." His special passion was for the intricacies, value, and history of high-performance Chevies: Trans-Ams, Camaros, and '68 'Vettes, which he'd overhaul for resale in California.

He drove a hard bargain but paid his bills promptly, in cash, kept his three tanks open to local fishermen and well stocked with Florida bass and black crappie, and kept his grass cut. When a neighboring farmer's combine broke, Koresh sent forty Davidians to harvest a whole field of moldering hay, then invited the farmer to swim in his pool. When company came they were regaled with an hour of songs and everyone ate. "I spent a fine afternoon with them last summer," says Mike Barnard, who runs a race-car machine shop deep in the woods beyond the compound. "Sitting by the pool, eating burgers, and fighting the fire ants. He ordered takeout from Fuddruckers. A hundred burgers and fries. He said I'd be amazed at the discount the fast-food places'll give when you order in numbers like that." When he bought supplies—five hundred diapers at the WalMart in Bellmead, $7,000 worth of groceries from the Sam's, three new engine blocks from Performance Automotive in Axtell, or bean-and-cheese nachos for a party of a dozen at Chelsea Street Pub when a good band was playing—he carried a money belt stuffed with thousands of dollars.

Among metalheads from local bands like Rif Raf, Flashback, and Blind Wolf, whom he'd meet at WhataBurger, Sunday barbecues, or a battle of the bands at the Cue Stick on the Old Dallas Highway, Koresh was known to "crack a cold Bud," "bird-dog the babes," and fantasize about "the ultimate band," which he'd get behind him and fly out to L.A. for meetings with music people. His business card, printed on heavy gold stock, read MESSIAH, a

Star of David dotting the *i*. He was fast, loud, could improvise
instantly with any song they threw at him, but nobody much liked
his music, which was too melodic and religious. They loved his
guitars, though: twenty-five, all air-brushed with detailed
paintings—a Star of David with fangs illustrating the points, the
ichthus, or a man sitting on a white horse, the white light of God's
love obscuring his features. His favorite showed a pair of boots
beside a tombstone at sundown: "a tribute" to the album *Passion
and Warfare* by guitarist Steve Vai, whom Koresh found "not religious but very spiritual." He wore it on his neck when, on slow
nights, he'd proselytize from the stage. A few kids went out for
all-night jams with cases of beer and buckets of popcorn and
returned to Mount Carmel for Bible studies, but only one joined
up, and he left after three months. "It got weird fast," singer
Jimbo Ward tells me. "Especially when you got your Lamb of God
telling the flock, 'You don't just shove your cock into her pussy.'"

To hunters, dealers, and weapons freaks at local gun shows,
where the T-shirts read I DON'T CALL 911 or GOD CREATED MEN,
SAM COLT MADE THEM EVEN, he was regarded as an equal, though
few could match his purchasing power and impulse buying: Koresh would think nothing of laying down $14,100 for two dozen
Colt AR-15 assault weapons, $1,300 for a Starlight infrared gun
scope, or $65 apiece for a gross of "hellfire switches," legal devices
to step up the rounds-per-minute of semiautomatic weapons.
When he fell in love with a 50-caliber bipod-mount semiautomatic
at a small Tennessee concern's booth at a Houston gun show last
year, he simply bought the gun and one hundred rounds of ammunition for $7,000 cash. Calling Jean Holub after the gun show,
Koresh told her, "Grandma, it's coming a time, I'm going to bring
you a little gun."

By the Saturday after the ATF raid, the press corps at Satellite
City has become a mile-long, $2-million-a-day tailgate party of
twelve-wheelers, prefab homes, camera towards, and sixty-foot
satellite dishes—"Twice the size," says BBC correspondent Gavin
Esler, "as for the Reykjavík summit." Soon the amenities are extended to include daily Fed Ex and U.S. mail deliveries, portable
toilets, and dedicated phone and electric lines. CNN, ever the
bigfoot on the block, has outfitted its Winnebago with a post-
modern suburban lawn of green felt and yard ornaments: ducks,
flamingos, a mailbox, Farmer and Mrs. Jones figures leaning over
a white picket fence. A Saturday-night dance is put on; a mayor,
running on "the Porta-Potti ticket," is elected; and identical-twin

cheerleaders are selling frozen yogurt at the corner near the final
checkpoint.

There's a strangely biblical feel to it, Texas-style. With a cold
snap and high winds in the first week, brightly colored tents are
staked down around the Salvation Army truck, where women in
plastic gloves dispense chipped-beef sandwiches and bowls of
beans and homemade boudin. The rumors percolating down
sound scriptural: Koresh has received thirty-six U.P.S. shipments
of plutonium, each for $36,000, COD. Koresh has decreed that
1,460 days after his trial and execution, authorities responsible
will suffer pestilence and locusts. Koresh has spent the previous
year tunneling his way to the superconducting supercollider up
in Waxahachie.

The banner from the watchtower looks like a beacon from a
boat stranded far out at sea. GOD HELP US WE NEED THE PRESS.
T-shirts soon appear at Satellite City—GOD HELP US WE ARE THE
PRESS—and it's clear that a ravenous symbiosis is at work. The FBI
feeds off the Davidians, who feed off the FBI; they both feed off
the press, who feed off absolutely everyone. And with each passing day, the explanation for being here seems to drift further
away.

Seven miles removed from this circus, on the road back toward Waco, what looks like a GMC floor show has amassed on
what is known as Holy Hill, a slight rise overlooking the vast,
beautiful meadow in which Mount Carmel sits. Started by T-shirt
hawkers, tourists, and a mother and daughter reading palms, it
quickly becomes the regional epicenter for the marginalized de-
vout. A pale, cross-bearing woman named Maraiah, who's failed
three times to enter Mount Carmel, has set up a station of the
cross/recycling center as far away from the money changers as
possible, and a Washington, D.C., man named Eddie McTwoHats
is beginning his recitation of "the longest song in history," about
David Koresh and the siege of Waco. A silk-suited preacher from
the House of David in Billings, Montana, is preaching that Koresh
is a true prophet but not the Lamb of God: "Revelation teaches
that the Lamb will only appear after the Seven Churches of Asia
are united. Saddam Hussein is the man who will do that."

Groups of evangelists and third-party politicos are displaying
graffiti likening the FBI and ATF agents to Nazi storm troopers,
asking IS YOUR RELIGION ATF-APPROVED? or warning of false
prophets: THE MOST DANGEROUS CULT LEADER—JOHN PAUL II, displayed by three renegade 1950s-looking Seventh-day Adventist

teens from Mount Vernon, Ohio, all wearing high-water pants, cardigan sweaters, and thick black-frame glasses. "The mark of the Beast," their leader, Fred Allback, tells me, "is Sunday observed as the Sabbath. That's just the Roman Catholic Church, in bed with the United States government."

One blistering Saturday, a fierce-looking man in a khaki suit, yellow T-shirt, a silver-and-gold Rolex Oyster, and tasseled loafers steps out of a Cadillac, two long-suffering men flanking him: The "God Said" Ministries' Pastor W. N. Otwell from Nacogdoches, a name in the state after a brief standoff that followed an arrest warrant for refusing to license a school run by his ministry, and a man feared by the listeners of his *Voice of Revolution* radio show. Come to argue for negotiations between the Davidians and some "real leader of men, not some 'pharaseetical' hypocrite from the FBI," he lapses into a diatribe on firearms, Luke 22, and Chelsea Clinton's enrollment in private school that has everyone thoroughly confused, heads nodding to the tempo of his inescapable logic. "I'm not a rock 'n' roll fan," he says, "but David reads out of the Bible and he can't be argued with. There are false prophets, but just where in the Bible does it say to take Satan with arms?"

Behind him, the Hallelujah Gang, three "traveling-along" evangelists out of Laredo, Texas, with chest-length beards of red, blond, and black, are talking about the wickedness at the end of the world, i.e., the incursion of federal and state forces on God-fearing communities like the FBI's siege of the Arm of the Lord compound in Arkansas, and the Weaver Family's eleven-day holdout in northern Idaho. "Governments always try to vindicate their evil. The Bible shows the kings and prophets in all their sin. Just like David. They say he's saying he's Jesus, but that's the FBI talking. C'mon. If he was Jesus, he wouldn't have to wait to hear from God, and he certainly wouldn't need automatic weapons to protect his people." As proof, they direct my eye to one of several dozen verses covering their Dodge Sportsman motor home: "The Saints overcame the Devil by the Blood of the Lamb and the Word of their testimony, and they loved their lives not unto death."

I walk with them over to the barbed-wire fence, where they point in the vague direction of Mount Carmel, not visible from here, then, five degrees over, to some points of light glistening in the noonday sun—the mobile-home city erected by the FBI 350 yards from David Koresh. "Mount Carmel," says Rick Long, the red-bearded one, "is where Elijah did battle with the prophets of

Ba'al. Just down from there," he moves his finger the five degrees to the FBI, "is where the final battle of Megiddo was waged."

"Megiddo?"

"Megiddo," he says, voice full of angry prophecy. "A harmless little town in the middle of nowhere, sometimes known with the prefix *har*. In later Scripture, that becomes Armageddon."

The lone star is flapping crazily at half-mast from the Star of David's flagpole by nightfall after the conflagration. Two days later a blue ATF banner is flying there as well. A pair of white Bobcat tractors is front-loading rubble from investigated areas into Dumpsters, and body parts are being excavated—ankles, palates, whole rib cages. A lot of bodies won't be identified: An arson specialist for the Waco fire marshal says the fire burned at upward of 500,000 BTUs and 2,400 degrees, enough to cremate. But amazingly, wildflowers and the spring grasses are growing twenty-five feet outside the rectangle of what was once Mount Carmel, and cows graze on all sides. It's as if the place were never here.

On Holy Hill, where business is booming, Jesse Amen, one of two men able to sneak past the FBI into Mount Carmel during the siege, tells of how David Koresh washed his feet when he entered Mount Carmel and presented him with a pair of boots when he left a month later. He gives them to Maraiah: gray half-tops with pointed toes and riding heels, soft sharkskin uppers, and leather conchos, which she offers to one and all, Cinderella-like, to see if they fit some new messiah.

At the FBI press conference three hours after the blaze, special agent Bob Ricks, the FBI's voice of temperance and patience for the past seven weeks, is clearly a man in crisis. His pronouncements now—calling Koresh "chicken" for not having blown himself up with hand grenades on the third day of the siege, and asserting, apparently falsely, that two surviving Davidians have admitted setting the fire—seem less like disinformation than an abject inability to fathom what's happened. A week later, more able to summon the righteousness of the lawman, he still betrays the illogic of dealing with people who "loved their lives not unto death" with the imperious logic of federal law: "All we can hope for," he says, equating the Davidians with the white-supremacist group the Order, one of whose members turned state's evidence, "is for sanity to take hold of one of these people."

The Vernon state hospital is six hours north of Waco. George Roden has been incarcerated there since 1990, when he was declared legally insane for killing a man he claims Koresh sent to kill him. Roden can perhaps provide an unorthodox but valid perspective on zealotry and why governments feel threatened by the intensely religious. He's agreed to see me if I bring organic nuts and apricots and a black Resistol cowboy hat: "Have 'em grease the crease," he tells me on the phone. "Leave the brim alone."

Accompanied by his psychiatrist, George receives me in a small anteroom of the hospital's high-security ward. For hours he talks only of his past and future ownership of the seventy-seven acres of Mount Carmel. Outside the window, high chain link fences are topped by loops of concertina wire. The Resistol doesn't fit George's head, but that doesn't bother him. He has Tourette Syndrome, and the generic medicine he gets at the hospital makes his hands shake uncontrollably. Some antipsychotic drug he can't remember the name of just now has dilated his pupils, and he seems to locate me out of the fog only occasionally. "The deed's in my name," he says. "It's as good as the State of Texas."

I ask if he knows that the Lone Star is flying at Mount Carmel now, and his hands clench into shaking fists. The psychiatrist leans forward preemptively. Is George aware that what he says may have legal consequences? he asks. The word *legal* brings a holy, derisive smile to George's lips. "The land's mine," he says. "I don't think any of the survivors are going to follow me. But when I get Mount Carmel back, I'm going to show the world what the Branch Davidians are all about."

At the end of a long afternoon, George's voice is still strong, his posture erect, and it's clear he could go on into the night, but the doctor says our time is up. As I leave the wing, he is being steadied down the hallway back to his room and more medication, ill-fitting black Resistol crammed down over his salt-and-pepper hair. In the end, George's hope and defiance don't mean much. He's stuck here in Vernon, a ward of the state, the last Davidian, all that remains of a religion.

As I race away from the hospital, dust devils are swirling amid the endless rocking-chair oil pumps and small Baptist churches along the north Texas prairie. Ahead, the sky is opening in a massive lightning show, and from behind comes a blue norther, blowing my car all over the road. This is tornado weather. You don't know when or where one's going to hit, or why. What a weatherman would call convection, some of the preachers on this road would describe as the wrath of God. To me, the gathering storm looks like one last revelation from Waco, but only a fool or a prophet would claim to understand it.

HOW DAVID KORESH GOT ALL
THOSE GUNS[3]

Only now is the size of David Koresh's arsenal coming into
focus. A thick computer printout in federal court in Waco, Texas,
reveals that the Ranch Apocalypse stockpile contained 59 handguns, 12 shotguns, 94 rifles and 45 machine guns; 1.8 million
rounds of ammunition; more than a dozen silencers; a variety of
hand grenade parts, and a hefty supply of other weapons compo-
nents. Among the inventory were two powerful .50-caliber Barrett rifles capable of hitting targets more than a mile away and
more than three dozen assault-style rifles such as AK-47s and
AR-15s.

How could Koresh assemble such an arsenal? The answer:
Pretty easily. For the better part of two years, Koresh avoided
much attention and deftly exploited gun laws to assemble his
arms cache, largely through gun shows and parcel delivery companies. Agents from the U.S. Bureau of Alcohol, Tobacco and
Firearms believe the Branch Davidians spent at least $199,715 on
weapons, ammo and related equipment between October 1991
and February 1993. Law-enforcement sources have identified a
total of 43 suppliers in 19 states who dealt with Koresh, and
virtually all the transactions were entirely legal. Those sources
believe Koresh initially identified many of the suppliers through a
publication called *Shotgun News,* which is a virtual Turkish bazaar
of the firearms trade. "People have the mistaken belief that the
federal government protects them from things like this," says
Josh Sugarmann of the nonprofit Violence Policy Center. "Most
people would be shocked that virtually anyone can legally assemble their own army in this country."

Authorities say Koresh and others like him skirt some provi-
sions of the law by purchasing gun parts rather than the completed weapons or by using legal parts to augment an existing
gun. For instance, manufacture of new machine guns, which fire
continuously with a single pull of the trigger and are also known
as automatic weapons, has been outlawed for civilian use since

[3]Article by George Witkin. From *U.S. News & World Report* 114: 42–43 Je 7 '93.
Copyright © 1993 by U.S. News & World Report. Reprinted with permission.

1986, as has possession of those guns. Kits that convert semi-automatic firearms—those that fire one shot for each pull of the trigger—into machine guns are also against the law, as is the conversion itself. But it is legal to sell "replacement parts" for machine guns manufactured before 1986. That means anyone with a little machining expertise and a few tools can combine the parts with a semiautomatic weapon to form an illegal machine gun.

ATF officials believe the majority of Koresh's machine guns were thus converted. The inventory of evidence compiled by the Texas Rangers in their search of the Davidians' compound included a metal lathe and two metal presses. Law-enforcement officials say at least 20 replacement-parts kits for the M-16 automatic rifle were sent to the Davidians by Tapco Inc. of Smyrna, Ga. Other M-16 kits came from a Barrington, Ill., firm, Nesard Gun Parts Co., whose owners had pleaded guilty to charges of transferring short-barreled rifles as part of a 1990 plea bargain arrangement. "Even though [they're] convicted felons," says an ATF affidavit, "they continue to conduct business because the company distributes gun parts and not firearms." A lawyer for the owners says they are "good people engaged in a lawful business."

Machine Gun

In addition, a former cultist told ATF agents that two cult members were using a computer program in an effort to design a primitive machine gun of their own known as a "grease gun." Koresh's attorney, Dick DeGuerin, says the Davidians did assemble guns from parts, but only because the process allowed them to turn a profit in reselling the weapons.

There is an especially troublesome loophole in gun law that allows hand grenades to circulate freely. No restriction exists on buying them so long as the explosive charge is not included. Investigation of the Davidians began after a box being delivered by a United Parcel Service employee broke open, revealing about 50 inert, pineapple-style grenades. Informants told ATF agents that Koresh was using such inert grenades, along with black powder and fuzes, to manufacture live grenades. Authorities maintain that the Davidians injured agents in the initial raid by hurling homemade hand grenades. Attorney DeGuerin says Koresh denied using hand grenades during the initial raid.

Koresh and his followers bought other weapons during frequent visits to Texas flea markets and gun shows. The ATF is overwhelmed in trying to regulate the hundreds of gun shows occurring nationwide each weekend, and critics like Sugarmann claim the shows "are like a Tupperware party for criminal gun traffickers."

Koresh obtained many guns, authorities say, through a federally licensed firearms dealer named Henry McMahon. McMahon says he sold Koresh about 225 guns in all, including AR-15s and AK-47s. He also accompanied Koresh to gun shows, providing guidance on the best available deals. As a federally licensed dealer, McMahon could get wholesale rates and order guns to be shipped interstate in quantity, without being subject to most record-keeping requirements. "If you've got access to a licensee, life gets much simpler," says one law-enforcement source. "They can stockpile any number of weapons in a short period of time without attracting attention."

McMahon traveled far and wide for his guns. Over one two-year period, he bought more than $100,000 worth of guns and equipment from Kiesler Police Supply Inc., a Jeffersonville, Ind., outlet that sells mostly to law-enforcement agencies. McMahon says Koresh accompanied him on a visit to Kiesler's in December 1991. "I have cried over this," says store president Doug Kiesler. "We're the friends of the police. But there's no crystal ball telling you a guy's a monster until he does something monstrous." McMahon says Koresh was a friend who was just "an average Joe." He says his gun sales to Koresh were all legal, and insists he has done nothing wrong.

The system for licensing dealers has come under increasing fire in recent months. Some 245,000 people own retail dealer's licenses, and obtaining one requires only $30 and a cursory criminal record check. A host of drug dealers and other criminals have been able to use fronts or take advantage of sloppy record-keeping in the system to get licenses and then amass arsenals. ATF can conduct only 20,000 dealer inspections a year.

A Friend Indeed

A federal indictment charges that another alleged Koresh lieutenant, Paul Fatta, was also a key weapons purchaser for the Davidians. An ATF affidavit states that Fatta bought three to five guns a week for the group starting in mid-1992, using funds from the 1989 sale of his Sacramento home. The affidavit says many of the guns were AR-15s, which Koresh preferred because they were easily convertible to machine guns. Fatta is in federal custody, charged with unlawfully conspiring to manufacture and possess unregistered machine guns. His attorney declines comment.

Gun-control activists believe the Waco tragedy gruesomely illustrates the need for new laws. Recently introduced bills would tighten requirements for federal firearms licenses and ban possession of certain assault-style weapons. Rep. Charles Schumer of New York, a leading gun-control advocate, is also planning introduction of a measure that would limit sales of replacement parts to those who own legally registered machine guns. Not surprisingly, the National Rifle Association doesn't think new laws are the answer. "If you're going to lay Waco off on the fact that firearms are available, I think you're on the wrong track," says NRA lobbyist James Baker. Agreement isn't likely anytime soon. The question is, while the two sides fiddle, will more Wacos burn?

A BOTCHED MISSION IN WACO, TEXAS[4]

Critics have tried to abolish it. Much of its mission involves ho-hum chores like preventing the sale of contraband cigarettes. It doesn't even have its own TV show.

But the Bureau of Alcohol, Tobacco and Firearms is a low-profile agency no more. After a Sunday-morning firefight at the 77-acre Branch Davidian compound outside Waco, Texas, that left four agents dead, 15 injured and an undetermined number of cult members dead or wounded, the ATF faces its own judgment day. Its bosses in the Treasury Department, Congress and the public are all aching to know how such a delicate mission could go so disastrously awry. "I think this was a very ineptly planned operation. It was carried out with the same unfortunate ineptitude," says Tony Cooper, a former Justice Department terrorism expert who now teaches courses in terrorism and conflict

[4]Article by James Popkin and Jeannye Thornton. From *U.S. News & World Report* 114:24–26 Mr 15 '93. Copyright © 1993 by U.S. News & World Report. Reprinted with permission.

resolution at the University of Texas at Dallas. Among the questions he and others ask:

• Why wasn't a less aggressive approach tried first? In 1988, when Branch Davidian leader David Koresh was charged in a shooting incident, he was taken into custody peacefully. The charges were eventually dismissed.

• Why weren't the compound's phones tapped? If they had been, authorities would have learned that a tipster had told Koresh about the raid.

• If officials feared Koresh's firepower and were counting on the element of surprise, why didn't they raid before dawn when most of the 100 or so sect members would have been sleeping?

• Why wasn't the undercover agent who had infiltrated the group ordered to stay in the compound to face arrest with the others? That would have kept his cover and, if the raid failed, would have allowed better monitoring of the sect.

"Ambushed"

Bureau officials argue that such second-guessing is unfair. Cult leader Koresh was "sworn to resistance," says bureau spokesman Jack Killorin, who contends it was only prudent to plan a raid backed by serious firepower. The *Houston Chronicle* reported late last week that Koresh met agents just before the gunfire began. "One of our guys said, 'Federal agents—put your hands up,'" one agent told the newspaper. "Koresh smiled, backed up and slammed the door. Almost immediately, within seconds, we were ambushed."

Although a wiretap might have helped prevent the slaughter, ATF spokesman Tom Hill says court officials would have rejected the request because the bureau could just as easily have received the wiretap information from its undercover agent. Bureau commanders also decided it was safe for its infiltrator to leave the compound, ATF Deputy Director Dan Hartnett says, because when he left "everything was normal." And Hill says ATF commanders decided to storm the ranch in the late morning because "that was the time when the children would come out to play and would be separated from the adults."

Despite such justifications, questions about the botched raid are fueling broader attacks on the ATF. Since overcoming efforts during the Reagan administration to abolish the agency and transfer its responsibilities to the Secret Service and the Customs Service, the bureau has expanded. Just 2,900 ATF employees were on the payroll in 1985; there are about 4,300 today. At the same time, the average age of ATF agents has decreased from 40 years to about 35. Josh Sugarmann of the Violence Policy Center claims the bureau has attempted to reshape its image to justify its growing budget and staff: "They like to be seen as the guys who kick in crack-house doors." Sugarmann wonders whether recent negative publicity—accusations that the ATF has turned a blind eye to sexual-harassment charges and was slow in promoting members of minority groups—might have influenced the decision to proceed with this high-profile raid.

The agency is in such turmoil, in fact, that some question its capacity to keep abreast of the growing menace of private arms caches. Not long ago, the business of collecting weapons arsenals was mostly the province of hate groups, survivalist sects and religious cults. Now experts say that such firepower is finding its way into the hands of lone citizens. "We get evidence of this when seemingly just ordinary folks are arrested," says Angie Lowery of Klanwatch.

On January 5, for example, police raided the home of Paterson, N.J., police Lt. William A. Van Kluyve and seized more than 100 pieces of semiautomatic weapons in a workshop, as well as pamphlets spelling out how to convert semiautomatic weapons into machine guns, and $97,000 in cash. Van Kluyve was charged with official misconduct and conspiracy to purchase prohibited weapons. In 1990, police in Ute, Iowa, seized $90,000 worth of illegal weapons, including a Thompson submachine gun, an AK-47, pistols, hand grenades and bayonets from Joseph Spencer, a former telephone company employee. He was arrested on weapons and drug charges. Police found white-supremacist propaganda in that raid, but Spencer did not seem to be affiliated with a hate group.

There are still plenty of such groups to worry officials. Jerry Wiedenhoff, a sergeant with the Kootenai County sheriff's office in Idaho, says weapons are rumored to be stockpiled on the Aryan Nation's 17-acre compound in Hayden Lake. Floyd Cochran, who defected from the group seven months ago, says he saw a smorgasbord of weapons and ammunition there, including AK-47 and SKS assault weapons. But the police department has never had probable cause to search the compound. Carl Franklin, the Aryan Nation's chief of staff, admits that he and individual

members own weapons, but he denies that the church is stockpiling.

Stockpiler

In 1989, the survivalist Church Universal and Triumphant in
Corwin Springs, Mont., was caught up in a weapons stockpiling
controversy. Edward Francis, husband of church leader Elizabeth
Clare Prophet, and the church's security officer were convicted of
conspiracy in buying nearly $150,000 worth of assault rifles and
more than 120,000 rounds of ammunition. Church spokesman
Murray Steinman says the pair acted without the sanction of
Prophet or the church.

Some worry that the events in Waco are a harbinger. "As we
get closer to the millennium, there will be more and more people
who will be arming themselves for the end of the world," predicts
sociologist James Aho at Idaho State University, author of "The
Politics of Righteousness." The problem is that ATF's handling of
the raid in Waco does not instill confidence that it is the best
agency to figure out what the proper responses should be.

TRIPPED UP BY LIES[5]

The elements are almost the stuff of comedy. Federal agents
get wind of a surreptitious arms hoard. They then set up surveillance of a compound using 40-year-old agents passing as college
students. Suddenly a raid on the compound is imminent—
without a detailed plan on how to carry it out. A sketchy plan is
then drawn up—and ignored. Meanwhile, the targets of the raid
know something is up, and their watchers know that the targets
know but still think surprise is a possibility. That's where the
comedy turns to tragedy.

"The decision to proceed was tragically wrong, not just in
retrospect, but because of what the decision makers knew at the
time." Thus concluded a devastating 220-page critique of the
Bureau of Alcohol, Tobacco and Firearms issued by the Treasury

[5]Article by Howard Chua-Eoan. From *Time* 142:39–40 O 11 '93. Copyright ©
1993 by Time, Inc. Reprinted with permission.

Department last week. The Feb. 28 [1993] raid on David Koresh's compound in Waco, Texas, resulted in the death of four ATF agents and six cult members and led to a 51-day siege and a fiery conflagration that claimed the lives of 85 people, including at least 17 children. The bureau, the report said, not only handled a sensitive situation ineptly but tried to cover up its bumbling with lies and obfuscations. As the study coldly noted, "There may be occasions when pressing operational considerations—or legal constraints—prevent law-enforcement officials from being . . . completely candid in their public utterances. This was not one of them."

After the report was released, Treasury Secretary Lloyd Bentsen, whose department is in charge of ATF, announced the replacement of the agency's entire top management. Its boss, Stephen Higgins, who knew the report was going to be harsh, announced his retirement three days before. "It is now clear that those in charge in Texas realized they had lost the element of surprise before the raid began," Bentsen said. The field commanders made "inaccurate and disingenuous statements" to cover up their missteps, putting the blame on agents.

ATF has had a tradition of going in with guns blazing. (For example, the legendary Eliot Ness and his Prohibition-era "Untouchables" were not FBI men, but rather direct predecessors of today's ATF agents.) The Branch Davidian saga was true to tradition. Little consideration was given to arresting David Koresh outside his Mount Carmel compound. Indeed, after its preliminary investigations, the ATF began preparing for what would be the biggest raid in its history. All it lacked was a plan—and the element of surprise. Even though a raid had been set for March 1, the mandatory documents for such a plan were not ready by Feb. 23. When acting Special Agent in Charge Darrell Dyer arrived from Kansas City and asked to see the paperwork, he found that none existed. In the next four days, Dyer and fellow agent William Krone drew up a plan—but it was never distributed. Meanwhile, Koresh was already suspicious, having noticed that the "college students" who had moved into a house near his 77-acre compound looked like people only a few years shy of their 25th reunion.

On the day of the raid, an ambulance company hired by the ATF agents leaked word of "Operation Trojan Horse" to a local TV station, which then sent a cameraman to check on the situation. The cameraman asked a local postman, David Jones, for directions to the Koresh compound. He also told Jones about the raid. Jones, who happened to be David Koresh's brother-in-law, told his father about the impending operation, and the word reached Koresh.

Koresh was leading a Bible session when he was tipped off. In attendance was Robert Rodriguez, an undercover ATF agent. Koresh was already suspicious of Rodriguez, but according to one surviving cult member had hoped to recruit him anyway. In a dramatic confrontation, said last week's report, Koresh, looking agitated, dropped his Bible and muttered the words "the kingdom of God." Then he said, "Neither the ATF team nor the National Guard will ever get me. They got me once and they'll never get me again." Looking out a window, he said, "They're coming, Robert. The time has come."

Rodriguez immediately made an excuse to leave in order to warn the ATF team that there was no longer any hope of surprise. As he headed out the door, Koresh grabbed his hand and said, "Good luck, Robert." The agent immediately reported to his superior, ATF tactical coordinator Charles Sarabyn, who relayed word to Phillip Chojnacki, the agent in charge of the raid. "Sarabyn expressed his belief that the raid could still be executed successfully if they hurried," said the report. "Chojnacki responded, 'Let's go.'" A number of agents informed the Treasury investigative panel that Sarabyn said things like "Get ready to go; they know we are coming."

ATF obfuscation began almost immediately after the compound burned down. On March 3 Daniel Hartnett, associate director of law enforcement, told the press that though Rodriguez knew Koresh had received a phone call, the agent "did not realize this was a tip at the time." On March 29 Higgins said, "We would not have executed the plans if our supervisors had lost the element [of surprise]."

When the Texas Rangers asked to see the plans for the raid, Chojnacki, Sarabyn and Dyer revised the original documents, says the report, "to make it more thorough and complete." Last week Bentsen summoned Hartnett, Chojnacki and Sarabyn, along with Edward Daniel Conroy, the deputy director for law enforcement, and David Troy, chief of the intelligence division, and told them they were being removed from active service. The evidence against them had been found in their own internal records and the accounts of more than 60 agents in the field.

ATF's future has already been much debated. Al Gore has

asked that it be dismembered, its firearms division merged with the FBI and the remaining sections sent over to the IRS. But Bentsen believes he has solved ATF's problems with the change of management. He will talk merger if the FBI agrees to preserve ATF's special knowledge of firearms. Also, some say, he would like the FBI to cede to the Secret Service more financial investigations. That is unlikely to happen.

While some reports indicate that a Justice Department report, expected this week, will rebuke lower- and mid-level FBI agents for the disastrous operation, sources have told *Time* that the criticisms will be relatively mild. In any case, the controversial question of mass suicide—and how carefully the FBI weighed it—is expected to be a large part of the report. The Treasury study indicated that the cult's self-destructive tendencies were already apparent in the first raid. Three of the cult fatalities were caused by gunshot wounds delivered at close range, indicating that they were suicides or executions.

II. ASSIGNING BLAME

EDITOR'S INTRODUCTION

That there was blundering in the ATF and FBI's handling of the Waco siege is beyond doubt. It is less clear whether the ultimate outcome could have been different. In the opening article of Section Two, James M. Wall in *Christian Century* contends that the ATF agents did not fully comprehend the apocalyptic mind set of Koresh and his followers. The ATF tear gas attack on the compound merely confirmed Koresh's embattled, end-of-the-world approach to religion. In the following article from *New York* magazine, John Taylor rejects the possibility that the FBI could ever have talked David Koresh into surrendering. Surrender would have meant the end of the cult, and long prison sentences, or even execution for some of the members. With their two-year supply of food, the Branch Davidians could have sustained themselves for a long time, and in the end, Taylor asserts, the final result would have been the same. Michael Barkun's article in *Christian Century* takes the position that the federal officers' worst mistake was the failure to take the cult's religious beliefs seriously. The Branch Davidian shows of force were a fulfillment of the vision of Armageddon that Koresh subscribed to and proceeded to act out. Barkun also discusses other "millenarian" groups in America, some who have caches of weapons and who may come into conflict with federal authorities as the year 2,000 (a point in time charged with special significance for seers and prophets) draws near.

EAGER FOR THE END[1]

Could the tragedy near Waco, Texas, have been avoided? What factors may have been overlooked in events that led to the

[1]Article by James M. Wall. From *Christian Century* 110:475–76 My 5 '93. Copyright © 1993 by the Christian Century Foundation. Reprinted with permission.

burning of the Branch Davidian compound, killing 86 people, including 17 young children? It is easy to second-guess officials performing under pressure. Working in full view of massive media coverage, law enforcement officials performed as best they could under the circumstances. But it must be noted that neither the Treasury Department officials, who conducted the initial raid on the compound, nor the FBI, which tried to unnerve a psychopathic personality with loud music and then gave him the opportunity to precipitate the blazing conclusion he wanted, seemed to comprehend the dangerousness of a charismatic psychopath who was immersed in apocalyptic literature.

Before questioning whether federal officials could have acted differently, we should recall that these officials entered a situation already heavily stacked against them. To begin with, they work in a society that makes it extremely easy for citizens to amass a supply of heavy weapons. The right to bear arms is the shibboleth that has enabled the National Rifle Association to enhance the arms industry and endanger society with the widespread availability of weapons. But the NRA presumes rationality on the part of gun owners and users. The apocalyptic world in which Koresh lived and with which he controlled his followers was not rational.

To the question in Revelation 5:2, "Who is worthy to open the book, and to loose the seals thereof?" David Koresh and his followers had an answer. He was the Lamb who could open the seals and precipitate the last days. So committed was his emotionally wounded band of followers to Koresh's leadership that they willingly turned over all sexual duties in the compound to him so that he might populate the world with his "seed." When Treasury agents launched their attack to disarm and arrest Koresh, he and his followers were ready. They resisted with the arms they had gathered for precisely this event. These were people with a worldview shaped by the imagery of "the Revelation of Jesus Christ, which God gave . . . to show unto his servants things which must shortly come to pass," things that God "sent and signified by his angel unto his servant John." If you are persuaded that none other than God is speaking, then a well-armed defense against Satan's force, not rationality, is the issue.

To the Davidians, the long siege that followed was proof that the final days were imminent. Satan was at hand. From his headquarters in Washington he had sent his agents to surround them. The final moment came when tanks stormed the compound, followed by choking tear gas that announced the end. This was no time to think of saving the children by sending them back into the world of Satan. It was time, instead, for the fire, and the promise of Revelation 21:6: "I will give unto him that is athirst of the fountain of the water of life freely."

We will never know how many of those who died were caught up in such rapturous thoughts; early indications are that not all of Koresh's followers were eager to die with him. Some may have been shot for trying to escape. But we may presume that Koresh and some of his "mighty warriors," the armed men who protected him as David's warriors protected their king, went willingly to their deaths. It is possible that they were so intoxicated by the imagery of Revelation that they went to their deaths believing that they had brought about "the new heaven and the new earth" (21:1).

Could this tragic ending have been different? We will never know, but we do know that well-intentioned law enforcement officials, operating under standard procedures, did not fully comprehend that they were dealing with a man with a dangerously narrow interpretation of apocalyptic literature. A passionate belief in the final days overrules all rational thought precisely because apocalypticism is not rational. It is the promise of the coming of the supernatural.

Since its controversial entry into the canon, Christians have differed over the meaning of the language in the Book of Revelation. Written, some believe, by a man named John who may have been the beloved disciple of Jesus, living and writing as an old man on the island of Patmos, the book inspires both conflict and hope. It becomes dangerous, however, when a belief in the final days becomes the sole object of devotion.

The imagery of Revelation, which scholars trace to an imaginative response to the harsh Roman rule of the first century, has a mesmerizing poetic power. When seen as a biblical promise for the New Jerusalem, apocalypticism may be a sustaining scriptural promise for the believer. But the bizarre imagery can also serve as a dangerous instrument of control in the hands of a charismatic leader.

The Waco tragedy has its roots in 1987 when the community that called itself the Branch Davidians accepted Vernon Howell as its leader, following his successful power struggles with the son of the founder of the original community. Changing his name to David Koresh (a reference, some think, to the Persian ruler Cyrus), the new leader shaped his group through a highly selective reading of Revelation and a twisted notion of himself as a messiah with absolute sexual control over his followers.

Jan Jarboe, a senior editor of *Texas Monthly*, describes Koresh as "a man who gorged on sex, beer, rock 'n' roll, guns and religion. The only holiness he saw was in himself. He justified sealing himself and his followers off in a concrete compound east of Waco by personifying himself as good and the rest of the world as evil." Koresh's followers were, Jarboe writes, people who "feel so empty and afraid, and disillusioned with families, the economy and politics that they are willing to pay almost any price for certainty."

Charges against Koresh related to the treatment of children had brought him to the attention of local law enforcement officials. Did the fact that he led a religious group delay an investigation into his behavior? Public officials tend to be uneasy when approaching individuals and groups that surround themselves with a religious aura. It is possible that without his religious cover, Koresh would have been subjected earlier to a more rigorous investigation. No interpretation of religious freedom is broad enough to have permitted these people to stockpile such a large collection of firearms within their tightly controlled compound.

In any event, Koresh's arms buildup, coupled with the belief that he was abusing children, prompted the Treasury Department's initial attack. When that attack failed, the 51-day siege began. These events provided a made-to-order scenario for a deranged leader ready to destroy himself and his followers to fulfill a mission. Did the attack that led to the final compound destruction come at the wrong time? Should the government have waited? Perhaps, but we have to consider that, as Attorney General Janet Reno maintains, the children in the compound were in danger for the simple reason that they were under the control of a disturbed man.

What should federal authorities have done with this gang of armed adults, who had already killed four federal agents and were holding 17 children hostage? How long is too long to wait, especially in light of allegations that Koresh had mistreated children in the past?

Law enforcement officials understandably treated Koresh as a thug and terrorist, but it was perhaps at this point they underestimated their opponent. Koresh was not so much a terrorist as he was a religious fanatic: he acted on the powerful conviction that he was following divine commands delivered to him in a book he and his followers believed to be literally written by God. Police

authorities consulted with religious scholars in their effort to respond to Koresh, but this consultation may not have gone far
enough. What was needed was not just a reading of the text that
Koresh had distorted, but a deeper understanding of the passion
that drives believers when they are convinced of the absolute
truth of their faith.

Government investigators will find little that is certain, except
that rational conversation and standard police hostage procedures are inadequate in dealing with an armed, self-designated
messiah. Koresh was willing to take his community to a fiery finish
because he was convinced that after the fire he would reveal
himself to the world as a risen messiah. In retrospect, it would
appear that a different strategy was needed, one that would have
avoided giving Koresh the apocalyptic scenario he wanted.

What remains obvious, however, is the ease with which Koresh
bought arms. It is also clear that local officials are uneasy in
approaching religious communities. These two factors were part
of the deadly combination that allowed Koresh to take his followers deep into the wild imagery of the Book of Revelation—a
document properly respected by believers, but easily distorted by
the deranged.

THE WACO BLAME GAME[2]

Second-Guessing the FBI

It's hard to think of an activity more psychically luxuriant
than second-guessing. It combines a maximum amount of self-
righteous moral indignation with irresistible opportunities to display intellectual superiority, a license for the unlimited criticism
of others, and absolutely no exposure to risk or responsibility. No
wonder then that second-guessing of the FBI's attempt to end the
standoff with the Branch Davidians reached a level of shrill feroc-
ity well before the flames that destroyed the cult's compound were
extinguished.

The original February 28 raid on the compound by agents of

[2]Article by John Taylor. From *New York* 26:10–12 My 3 '93. Copyright © 1993
by New York. Reprinted with permission.

the Bureau of Alcohol, Tobacco, and Firearms had unquestionably been bungled. That debacle created a narrative premise: that buffoonish Feds and crazed cult members were together acting out some sort of black farce in the trashy trailer-park-gothic setting of rural Texas. The premise was reinforced by subsequent developments. David Koresh's shameless greed for publicity, his biblical rantings, and his increasingly preposterous demands (a word processor to complete an analysis of the Seven Seals), combined with the surreal appearance of tanks and helicopters, with loudspeakers belting out "Jingle Bell Rock" and recordings of rabbits being slaughtered, while lawyers hawked book rights, made for a satirical techno-pop extravaganza.

The situation was far wilder than anything Robert Altman ever dared to conceive. But just as it began to seem too ridiculous for words, it ended, abruptly and tragically. There was no time for mourning, however—except perhaps at a few church services in Waco—no letup in the overwrought media cyclone, and thus little opportunity for most people to pause and actually experience their feelings about the death by fire of 17 children and 69 adults. Instead, the farce of the standoff was immediately supplanted by the equally hysterical farce of, to use a phrase George Bush popularized last year, "the blame game."

Some in the press approached this task with a gusto that bordered on joy. The idea about FBI culpability in the immolation of the cultists fulfilled not only the original narrative premise of the siege (bumbling Feds) but also the more general, reflexive skepticism liberal journalists have had of federal law-enforcement agents. The tradition, ever since the sixties, has been to romanticize outlaws while disparaging the FBI as an enemy of social progress, the very embodiment of reactionary authority. Its members were all thought to wear black Corfam shoes and white socks. Their malice was supposed to be exceeded only by their incompetence. In Waco, according to those who subscribed to this view, they had once again made utter fools of themselves.

While most of the public, in an initial poll, agreed with Bill Clinton that David Koresh had killed his followers, the members of the press tended to blame the FBI. The Bureau had "provoked" Koresh, they felt. It had "triggered" his action. Koresh, after all, couldn't be held responsible because he was insane, and his followers couldn't be held responsible because they were in his thrall. If the FBI had treated Koresh with the patience and understanding that the insane deserve, the tragedy could have been averted.

Instead, federal agents, in a fit of macho pique because he had successfully thwarted them, *drove* the cult leader to start the fire. In this scenario, Koresh becomes almost as much a victim as the children, his decision to ignite the compound an incidental act in a series of events he did not initiate. (It seems safe to assume, despite denials from the survivors, that Koresh did burn the place down. Federal agents saw people apparently lighting the fire. It seemed to begin in several places, and engulfed the entire building almost immediately.)

But what was in fact incidental to the tragic outcome was the FBI's decision to take action. It merely provided Koresh with the pretext he had been looking for to destroy himself and his followers. The idea that Koresh could have been talked into surrendering at some point in the future is not supported by the facts. He and his followers knew they had murdered four federal agents and wounded sixteen others. They were aware that if they surrendered, the cult would be broken up, many of them would be given long prison terms, and, since this was Texas, a few would probably be sentenced to death and executed. That clearly had no appeal.

What did seem appealing was an indefinite state of siege. It invested the cultists' daily routine with intensity and satisfied their collective persecution complex. Their attitude toward the federal agents who surrounded them was increasingly casual, almost blasé; cultists, who had kept indoors after the first shoot-out, took to strolling outside the compound walls and appearing on the roof to smoke cigarettes. The discomfort they endured was minimal. They had, according to the FBI, up to two years' supply of food. They had their own source of water. They had their 104 assault rifles, their grenade launcher, their 8,000 rounds of ammunition.

Many of the cultists' relatives have faulted the FBI for not arranging for them to talk to their family members inside the compound, but it's highly unlikely that Koresh would have allowed his followers to get on the telephone with their relatives, who would encourage them to desert. A cult leader's hold over his followers exists in inverse proportion to their contacts with the rest of society.

It is true that if the FBI had not moved in on April 19, the cultists and their children would be alive today. But because that date had a certain arbitrariness does not mean the decision to take action was wrong. Such specifics almost always have an arbitrary quality. The alternative was not to take action on some less arbitrary occasion—since Koresh was becoming more erratic and the talks with him were regressing rather than progressing, the prospects for a negotiated settlement were dwindling—but to take no action.

That would have been the advice of the cult experts who, in the days after the conflagration, faulted the FBI for failing to consult with *them*. But the ensuing standoff could have lasted as long as two years. It would have allowed Koresh to flout the country's laws, setting up his own rogue kingdom within the national borders. And it, too, could just as easily have ended in tragedy. "Do we wait 90 more days until the children die?" asked Jeff Jamar, the FBI agent in charge of the siege. "How would the federal government look when we finally get into the compound [if] there are children dying of hunger, children dying of disease because of the conditions?"

In the accusatory deluge that has followed the fire, it's been easy to forget that the federal agents were on a rescue mission. While they did not have, as they first suggested, a sheaf of new reports of child abuse, they nonetheless had legitimate reason to be alarmed about the children. The old reports were persuasive. And conditions in the compound were unsanitary. According to Justice Department spokesman Carl Stern, human waste was being thrown out the compound doors in pails.

The charge has been made that the FBI acted out of "impatience," suggesting that judgment had lapsed into emotionalism. In fact, agents showed restraint throughout the operation. They adhered to the policy of "no return fire," even though as they moved in on the compound, the cultists fired some 80 rounds at them.

Attorney General Janet Reno has admitted that everyone failed to anticipate the mass suicide. But failure to anticipate someone's decision to commit suicide does not translate into responsibility for it. That Koresh was intent all along on killing himself and his followers and their children if he had to leave the compound is evident from the fact that this is what occurred. As happened in Jonestown, it was the unavoidable dissolution of the cult, brought on by the crimes committed at the leader's instigation, that led the leader to order the death of his followers. Some of them, according to reports circulating in Waco, may have been killed by Koresh's "Mighty Men" before the fire started.

The tank muzzle punching through the flimsy compound

wall was only the proximate cause of the catastrophe. The FBI's
mistakes were procedural rather than fundamental. If its agents
are truly guilty of anything, it is the guilt of those unable to
prevent the inevitable.

REFLECTIONS AFTER WACO:
MILLENNIALISTS AND THE STATE[3]

Not since Jonestown has the public been so gripped by the
conjunction of religion, violence and communal living as they
have by the events at the Branch Davidians' compound. All that
actually took place near Waco remains unknown or contested.
Nonetheless, the information is sufficient to allow at least a preliminary examination of three questions: Why did it happen?
Why didn't it happen earlier? Will it happen again?

As a *New York Times* editorialist put it, "The Koresh affair has
been mishandled from beginning to end." The government's
lapses, errors and misjudgments can be grouped into two main
categories: issues of law-enforcement procedure and technique,
with which I do not propose to deal; and larger issues of strategy
and approach, which I will address.

The single most damaging mistake on the part of federal
officials was their failure to take the Branch Davidians' religious
beliefs seriously. Instead, David Koresh and his followers were
viewed as being in the grip of delusions that prevented them from
grasping reality. As bizarre and misguided as their beliefs might
have seemed, it was necessary to grasp the role these beliefs
played in their lives; these beliefs were the basis of *their* reality.
The Branch Davidians clearly possessed an encompassing worldview to which they attached ultimate significance. That they did
so carried three implications. First, they could entertain no other
set of beliefs. Indeed, all other views of the world, including those
held by government negotiators, could only be regarded as erroneous. The lengthy and fruitless conversations between the two

[3]Article by Michael Barkun, professor of political science, Syracuse University.
From *Christian Century* 110:596–600 Je 2 '93. Copyright © 1993 by the Christian
Century Foundation. Reprinted with permission.

sides were, in effect, an interchange between different cultures—they talked past one another.

Second, since these beliefs were the basis of the Branch Davidians' sense of personal identity and meaning, they were non-negotiable. The conventional conception of negotiation as agreement about some exchange or compromise between the parties was meaningless in this context. How could anything of ultimate significance be surrendered to an adversary steeped in evil and error? Finally, such a belief system implies a link between ideas and actions. It requires that we take seriously—as apparently the authorities did not—the fact that actions might be based on something other than obvious self-interest.

Conventional negotiation assumes that the parties think in terms of costs and benefits and will calculate an outcome that minimizes the former and maximizes the latter. In Waco, however, the government faced a group seemingly impervious to appeals based upon interests, even where the interests involved were their own life and liberty. Instead, they showed a willingness to take ideas to their logical end-points, with whatever sacrifice that might entail.

The Branch Davidians did indeed operate with a structure of beliefs whose authoritative interpreter was David Koresh. However absurd the system might seem to us, it does no good to dismiss it. Ideas that may appear absurd, erroneous or morally repugnant in the eyes of outsiders continue to drive believers' actions. Indeed, outsiders' rejection may lead some believers to hold their views all the more tenaciously as the group defines itself as an island of enlightenment in a sea of error. Rejection validates their sense of mission and their belief that they alone have access to true knowledge of God's will.

These dynamics assumed particular force in the case of the Branch Davidians because their belief system was so clearly millenarian. They anticipated, as historian Norman Cohn would put it, total, immediate, collective, imminent, terrestrial salvation. Such commitments are even less subject than others to compromise, since the logic of the system insists that transcendent forces are moving inexorably toward the fulfillment of history.

Federal authorities were clearly unfamiliar and uncomfortable with religion's ability to drive human behavior to the point of sacrificing all other loyalties. Consequently, officials reacted by trying to assimilate the Waco situation to more familiar and less threatening stereotypes, treating the Branch Davidians as they would hijackers and hostage-takers. This tactic accorded with the very human inclination to screen out disturbing new events by pretending they are simply variations of what we already know. Further, to pretend that the novel is really familiar is itself reassuring, especially when the familiar has already provided opportunities for law–enforcement officials to demonstrate their control and mastery. The FBI has an admirable record of dealing effectively with hijackers and hostage-takers; therefore, acting as if Waco were such a case encouraged the belief that here too traditional techniques would work.

The perpetuation of such stereotypes at Waco, as well as the failure to fully appreciate the religious dimension of the situation, resulted in large measure from the "cult" concept. Both the authorities and the media referred endlessly to the Branch Davidians as a "cult" and Koresh as a "cult leader." The term "cult" is virtually meaningless. It tells us far more about those who use it than about those to whom it is applied. It has become little more than a label slapped on religious groups regarded as too exotic, marginal or dangerous.

As soon as a group achieves respectability by numbers or longevity, the label drops away. Thus books on "cults" published in the 1940s routinely applied the term to Christian Scientists, Jehovah's Witnesses, Mormons and Seventh-day Adventists, none of whom are referred to in comparable terms today. "Cult" has become so clearly pejorative that to dub a group a "cult" is to associate it with irrationality and authoritarianism. Its leaders practice "mind control," its members have been "brainwashed" and its beliefs are "delusions." To be called a "cult" is to be linked not to religion but to psychopathology.

In the Waco case, the "cult" concept had two dangerous effects. First, because the word supplies a label, not an explanation, it hindered efforts to understand the movement from the participants' perspectives. The very act of classification itself seems to make further investigation unnecessary. To compound the problem, in this instance the classification imposed upon the group resulted from a negative evaluation by what appear to have been basically hostile observers. Second, since the proliferation of new religious groups in the 1960s, a network of so-called "cult experts" has arisen, drawn from the ranks of the academy, apostates from such religious groups, and members' relatives who have become estranged from their kin because of the "cult" affiliations. Like many other law–enforcement agencies, the FBI has relied heavily on this questionable and highly partisan expertise—with tragic consequences. It was tempting to do so since the hostility of those in the "anti–cult" movement mirrored the authorities' own anger and frustration.

These cascading misunderstandings resulted in violence because they produced erroneous views of the role force plays in dealing with armed millenarians. In such confrontations, dramatic demonstrations of force by the authorities provoke instead of intimidate. It is important to understand that millenarians possess a "script"—a conception of the sequence of events that must play out at the end of history. The vast majority of contemporary millenarians are satisfied to leave the details of this script in God's hands. Confrontation can occur, however, because groups often conceive of the script in terms of a climactic struggle between forces of good and evil.

How religious prophecy is interpreted is inseparable from how a person or a group connects events with the millenarian narrative. Because these believers' script emphasizes battle and resistance, it requires two players: the millenarians as God's instruments or representatives, and a failed but still resisting temporal order. By using massive force the Bureau of Alcohol, Tobacco and Firearms on February 28, and the FBI on April 19, unwittingly conformed to Koresh's millenarian script. He wanted and needed their opposition, which they obligingly provided in the form of the initial assault, the nationally publicized siege, and the final tank and gas attack. When viewed from a millenarian perspective, these actions, intended as pressure, were the fulfillment of prophecy.

The government's actions almost certainly increased the resolve of those in the compound, subdued the doubters and raised Koresh's stature by in effect validating his predictions. Attempts after the February 28 assault to "increase the pressure" through such tactics as floodlights and sound bombardment now seem as pathetic as they were counterproductive. They reflect the flawed premise that the Branch Davidians were more interested in calculating costs and benefits than in taking deeply held beliefs to their logical conclusions. Since the government's own actions seemed to support Koresh's teachings, followers had little incentive to question them.

The final conflagration is even now the subject of dispute between the FBI, which insists that the blazes were set, and survivors who maintain that a tank overturned a lantern. In any case, even if the FBI's account proves correct, "suicide" seems an inadequate label for the group's fiery demise. Unlike Jonestown, where community members took their own lives in an isolated setting, the Waco deaths occurred in the midst of a violent confrontation. If the fires were indeed set, they may have been seen as a further working through of the script's implications. It would not have been the first time that vastly outnumbered millenarians engaged in self-destructive behavior in the conviction that God's will required it. In 1525, during the German Peasants' Revolt, Thomas Münzer led his forces into a battle so hopeless that 5,000 of his troops perished, compared to six fatalities among their opponents.

Just as the authorities in Waco failed to understand the connections between religion and violence, so they failed to grasp the nature of charismatic leadership. Charisma, in its classic sociological sense, transcends law and custom. When a Dallas reporter asked Koresh whether he thought he was above the law, he responded: "I *am* the law." Given such self-perception, charismatic figures can be maddeningly erratic; they feel no obligation to remain consistent with pre-existing rules. Koresh's swings of mood and attitude seemed to have been a major factor in the FBI's growing frustration, yet they were wholly consistent with a charismatic style.

Nevertheless, charismatic leaders do confront limits. One is the body of doctrine to which he or she is committed. This limit is often overcome by the charismatic interpreter's ingenuity combined with the texts' ambiguity (Koresh, like so many millennialists, was drawn to the vivid yet famously obscure language of the Book of Revelation).

The other and more significant limit is imposed by the charismatic leader's need to validate his claim to leadership by his performance. Charismatic leadership is less a matter of inherent talents than it is a complex relational and situational matter between leader and followers. Since much depends on followers' granting that a leader possesses extraordinary gifts, the leader's claim is usually subject to repeated testing. A leader acknowledged at one time may be rejected at another. Here too the Waco incident provided an opportunity for the authorities inadvertently to meet millenialist needs. The protracted discussions with Koresh and his ability to tie down government resources gave the impression of a single individual toying with a powerful state. While to the outer world Koresh may have seemed besieged, to those in the community he may well have provided ample evidence of his power by immobilizing a veritable army of law—enforcement personnel and dominating the media.

Given the government's flawed approach, what ought to have been done? Clearly, we will never know what might have resulted from another strategy. Nonetheless, taking note of two principles might have led to a very different and less violent outcome. First, the government benefited more than Koresh from the passage of time. However ample the Branch Davidians' material stockpiles, these supplies were finite and diminishing. While their resolve was extraordinary, we do not know how it might have been tested by privation, boredom and the eventual movement of public and official attention to other matters. Further, the longer the time that elapsed, the greater the possibility that Koresh in his doctrinal maneuvering might have constructed a theological rationalization that would have permitted surrender. Messianic figures, even those cut from seemingly fanatic cloth, have occasionally exhibited unpredictable moments of prudential calculation and submission (one thinks, for example, of the sudden conversion to Islam of the 17th-century Jewish false messiah Sabbatai Zevi). Time was a commodity the government could afford, more so than Koresh, particularly since a significant proportion of the community's members were almost certainly innocent of directly violating the law.

As important as patience, however, would have been the government's willingness to use restraint in both the application and the appearance of force. The ATF raid, with its miscalculations and loss of life, immediately converted a difficult situation into one fraught with danger. Yet further bloodshed might have been averted had authorities been willing both to wait and to avoid a dramatic show of force. Federal forces should have been rapidly drawn down to the lowest level necessary to prevent individuals from leaving the compound undetected. Those forces that remained should have been as inconspicuous as possible. The combination of a barely visible federal presence, together with a willingness to wait, would have accomplished two things: it would have avoided government actions that confirmed apocalyptic prophecies, and it would have deprived Koresh of his opportunity to validate his charismatic authority through the marathon negotiations that played as well-rehearsed millenarian theater. While there is no guarantee that these measures would have succeeded (events within the compound might still have forced the issue),

they held a far better chance of succeeding than the confronta-
tional tactics that were employed.

The events in Waco were not the first time in recent years that
a confrontation between a communal group and government
forces has ended in violence. Several years ago the Philadelphia
police accidentally burned down an entire city block in their attempt to evict the MOVE sect from an urban commune. In 1985
surrender narrowly averted a bloody confrontation at Zarephath-
Horeb, the heavily armed Christian Identity community in Mis-
souri organized by the Covenant, Sword and Arm of the Lord. In
August 1992 a federal raid on the Idaho mountaintop cabin of a
Christian Identity family resulted in an 11-day armed standoff
and the deaths of a U.S. marshal and two family members. In this
case, too, the aim was the arrest of an alleged violator of firearms
law, Randy Weaver, whose eventual trial, ironically, took place
even as the FBI prepared its final assault on the Branch Davidians. In retrospect, the Weaver affair was Waco in microcosm—
one from which, apparently, the ATF learned little.

These cases, which should have been seen to signal new forms
of religion-state conflict, were untypical of the relationships with
government enjoyed by earlier communal societies. While a few
such groups, notably the Mormons, were objects of intense violence, most were able to arrive at some way of living with the
established order. Many, like the Shakers, were pacifists who had
a principled opposition to violence. Some, like the German pietist
sects, were primarily interested in preserving their cultural and
religious distinctiveness; they only wanted to be left alone. Still
others, such as the Oneida perfectionists, saw themselves as models of an ideal social order—exemplars who might tempt the
larger society to reform. In all cases, an implied social contract
operated in which toleration was granted in exchange for the
community's restraint in testing the limits of societal acceptance.
When external pressure mounted (as it did in response to the
Oneida Community's practice of "complex marriage"), commu-
nitarians almost always backed down. They did so not because
they lacked religious commitment, but because these communities placed such a high value on maintaining their separate
identities and on convincing fellow citizens that their novel social
arrangements had merit.

The Branch Davidians clearly were not similarly motivated,
and it is no defense of the government's policy to acknowledge
that Koresh and his followers would have sorely tested the pa-

tience of any state. Now that the events of Waco are over, can we say that the problem itself has disappeared? Are armed millenarians in America likely to be again drawn or provoked into violent conflict with the established order? The answer, unfortunately, is probably yes. For this reason Waco's lessons are more than merely historically interesting.

The universe of American communal groups is densely populated—they certainly number in the thousands—and it includes an enormous variety of ideological and religious persuasions. Some religious communities are millenarian, and of these some grow out of a "posttribulationist" theology. They believe, that is, that Armageddon and the Second Coming will be preceded by seven years of turmoil (the tribulation), but they part company with the dominant strain of contemporary Protestant millennialism in the position they assign to the saved. The dominant millenarian current (dispensational premillennialism) assumes that a Rapture will lift the saved off the earth to join Christ before the tribulation begins, a position widely promulgated by such televangelists as Jerry Falwell. Posttribulationists, on the other hand, do not foresee such a rescue and insist that Christians must endure the tribulation's rigors, which include the reign of the Antichrist. Their emphasis upon chaos and persecution sometimes leads them toward a "survivalist" lifestyle—retreat into defendable, self-sufficient rural settlements where they can, they believe, wait out the coming upheavals.

Of all the posttribulationists, those most likely to ignite future Wacos are affiliated with the Christian Identity movement. These groups, on the outermost fringes of American religion, believe that white "Aryans" are the direct descendants of the tribes of Israel, while Jews are children of Satan. Not surprisingly, Identity has become highly influential in the white supremacist right. While its numbers are small (probably between 20,000 and 50,000), its penchant for survivalism and its hostility toward Jews and nonwhites renders the Christian Identity movement a likely candidate for future violent conflict with the state.

When millenarians retreat into communal settlements they create a complex tension between withdrawal and engagement. Many communal societies in the 19th century saw themselves as showcases for social experimentation—what historian Arthur Bestor has called "patent office models of society." But posttribulationist, survivalist groups are defensive communities designed to keep at bay a world they despise and fear. They often deny the legitimacy of government and other institutions. For some, the reign of Antichrist has already begun. To white supremacists, the state is ZOG—the Zionist Occupation Government. For them, no social contract can exist between themselves and the enemy—the state. Their sense of besiegement and their links to paramilitary subcultures virtually guarantee that, no matter how committed they may be to lives of isolation, they will inevitably run afoul of the law. The flash-point could involve firearms regulations, the tax system, or the treatment of children.

These and similar groups will receive a subtle but powerful cultural boost as we move toward the year 2000. Even secularists seem drawn, however irrationally, toward the symbolism of the millennial number. The decimal system invests such dates with a presumptive importance. We unthinkingly assume they are watersheds in time, points that divide historical epochs. If even irreligious persons pause in expectation before such a date, is it surprising that millennialists do so? As we move closer to the year 2000, therefore, millenarian date-setting and expectations of transformation will increase.

If this prognosis is valid, what should government policy be toward millennial groups? As I have suggested, government must take religious beliefs seriously. It must seek to understand the groups that hold these beliefs, rather than lumping the more marginal among them in a residual category of "cults." As Waco has shown, violence is a product of interaction and therefore may be partially controlled by the state. The state may not be able to change a group's doctrinal propensities, but it can control its own reactions, and in doing so may exert significant leverage over the outcome. The overt behavior of some millenarian groups will undoubtedly force state action, but the potential for violence can be mitigated if law-enforcement personnel avoid dramatic presentations of force. If, on the other hand, they naïvely become co-participants in millenarians' end-time scripts, future Wacos will be not merely probable; they will be inevitable. The government's inability to learn from episodes such as the Weaver affair in Idaho provides little cause for short-term optimism. The lesson the ATF apparently took from that event was that if substantial force produced loss of life, then in the next case even more force must be used. Waco was the result.

Admittedly, to ask the government to be more sensitive to religious beliefs in such cases is to raise problems as well as to solve them. It raises the possibility of significant new constitutional questions connected with the First Amendment's guarantee of the free exercise of religion. If the state is not to consign all new and unusual religious groups to the realm of outcast "cults," how is it to differentiate among them? Should the state monitor doctrine to distinguish those religious organizations that require particularly close observation? News reports suggest that Islamic groups may already be the subjects of such surveillance—a chilling and disturbing prospect. Who decides that a group is dangerous? By what criteria? If beliefs can lead to actions, and if those actions violate the law, how should order and security be balanced against religious freedom? Can belief be taken into account without fatally compromising free exercise?

These are difficult questions for which American political practice and constitutional adjudication provide little guidance. They need to be addressed, and soon. In an era of religious ferment and millennial excitation, the problems posed by the Branch Davidians can only multiply.

III. THE CULT'S CHILDREN

EDITOR'S INTRODUCTION

The endangered welfare of children in the Branch Davidian cult played an influential role in the government's decision to strike. The cult child as victim is addressed in the several articles that follow. Sophfronia Scott Gregory in *Time* discusses the psychiatric report on children who had lived in the compound. To ensure his control, Koresh undermined family attachments so that all relationships centered upon himself. Children were usually separated from their mothers and fathers by age twelve—the boys to endure a regimen that involved getting up at 5:30 a.m., the girls to be singled out as Koresh's sex partners. Ginny Carroll and Melinda Beck, writing in *Newsweek*, discuss the twenty-one children (from age 5 months to 12 years) who, after the initial shoot-out in February, were released into the custody of the Texas child welfare agency. The authors speculate on their chances of leading normal lives. In the following article, from *Newsweek*, David Gelman points out that the children are likely to suffer from some of the same symptoms of Post-Traumatic Stress Disorder as Vietnam combat veterans have. These children are expected to experience nightmares and "psychic numbing" as time goes on. There is also concern that they—repeating a well-documented pattern—may in fact become child abusers and wife-beaters as adults.

CHILDREN OF A LESSER GOD[1]

Her new home looked warm and welcoming enough to the young Branch Davidian girl. She was fascinated with the hot running water, flush toilets, heated food. The Waco compound had

[1]Article by Sophronia Scott Gregory. From *Time* 141:54 My 17 '93. Copyright © 1993 by Time, Inc. Reprinted with permission.

no such comforts. But upon passing a door leading to the base-
ment, the youngster froze. "Do you have a whipping room down
there?" she asked her new guardians. "No," answered the woman
who now cared for her, "do you have one?" "Yes," said the little
girl. "When they don't want everyone to hear us, they take us
down there."

With the sect consumed by fire, the tales of life in Mount
Carmel come mostly out of the mouths of babes. As stories from
survivors, former Davidians and a psychiatric report on the children confirmed last week, the Ranch Apocalypse experience was
one of deprivation and fear. Denied traditional family bonds and
exposed to Koresh's warped teachings, the children became compliant playthings, expected to live by every word issuing from the
mad messiah of Waco.

When young Davidians strayed from his commands, their
punishment was severe (though one survivor insisted such redress
was basic "Christian discipline"). Disobedience frequently
brought out the "helper," a paddle often wielded by Koresh's
"mighty men" in the "whipping room" just off the first floor. The
instrument left circle-shaped lesions, an inch across, on the children's buttocks. Koresh's son Cyrus, when he was three years old,
once refused a command and, according to a former cult member, was starved for two days and forced to sleep on a garage floor
where Koresh told him large rats prowled.

By age 12, children were usually split off from their mothers
(fathers never lived with the families). Brothers and sisters were
separated to live with other same-sex companions. They ate fruits
and vegetables, but rarely warm food. Chocolate was prohibited,
and ice cream, which Koresh enjoyed regularly, was granted only
occasionally to the children. The boys were awakened at 5:30 a.m.
for "gym," a series of paramilitary marching and drills; in addition, fights between the boys were staged possibly in preparation
for man-to-man combat in an apocalyptic war. If they did not
participate vigorously enough, discipline followed. Girls were
spared the training and could sleep as late as they wanted, but
they did have to help empty human waste from the white plastic
pails used as toilets by the sect members.

To ensure his control, Koresh undermined family attachments. The children were told to consider him their only father—
their parents were called "dogs." When psychiatrists later asked
for drawings of their families, the confused children sketched
clusters of "favorite" people. "One of the most disturbing quali-

ties observed in the children . . . was the . . . apparent weakness in their attachments to adults (sometimes including parents) in or out of the compound," says Bruce Perry, the Baylor College of Medicine psychiatrist who headed the team of 12 medical volunteers that studied the children for two months following the Feb. 28 raid.

Education consisted of home schooling and hours-long twice-daily biblical lessons taught by a rambling Koresh. Sometimes he jumped from the chapel stage to paddle young ones who were crying or being disruptive. "You never knew what he was going to be," says Kiri Jewell, 12, who was taken from the compound by her natural father in 1991. "One minute he was nice, and the next he was suddenly nasty." The children also learned songs filled with violent apocalyptic imagery. War and martial-arts films proliferated in the cult's video library. Koresh preached that the world was full of "bad guys," hurtful unbelievers out to kill the Davidians. Mistrust everyone, he said; deceive all nonbelievers. At Waco's Methodist Home, where the compound children were housed following their release, Perry, carrying a five-month-old child, was approached by a small girl. "Did you come here to kill the baby?" she asked him.

Girls were singled out early as Koresh's sex-partners-to-be. Some as young as 11 wore a plastic Star of David around their neck, while others wore a thin gold band on their finger. Koresh spoke openly about the details of sex to prepare them for intercourse. "Sexual themes were associated with pleasing Koresh," says Perry, "and procreating [to fill] the earth with his glorious seed."

All but four of the 21 surviving children have been placed with parents and relatives. Yet Koresh still looms as an ambivalent shadow, a daunting memory. In their drawings the compound is both riddled with bullet holes and depicted as the kingdom of heaven. In other drawings, they surrounded the words I LOVE DAVID with hearts. "They learned to substitute the word love for fear," Perry told the New York *Times*. Living a normal life will not be easy. "We were all waiting for the end to happen," says Kiri Jewell. It has—and now life must go on.

CHILDREN OF THE CULT[2]

Late on the last Sunday in February, the first young refugees from the Branch Davidian cult arrived at the Methodist Home for children in Waco, Texas. The staff and extra volunteers were on call, beds were freshly made, snacks at hand if the youngsters needed a comforting cookie or two. But someone had left the television on, and as the first little girl walked into the living room, the image on the screen turned violent. Jack Daniels, president of the home, reached across and snapped off the set. "Oh," said the little girl surprised at his caution. "We watch TV. We watch war movies." Daniels froze in her innocent stare. "We were trying to protect her," he says, still startled two months later, "and she's talking about war movies."

"Platoon," as it turned out, wasn't the half of it. She and the others had stepped out through the looking glass. Away from a world where apocalyptic visions were fulfilled in a deadly fire fight with federal agents. Away from the Orwellian reign of a charismatic, iron-willed prophet who demanded obedience, faith and the sexual favors of 12-year-old girls. And away from a world that, despite obvious deprivation and harsh discipline was also filled with joy and affection and the adults she and the others loved and trusted.

Many mysteries of Branch Davidian life will remain lost forever in the charred rubble of Ranch Apocalypse. But last week stories began to emerge about what life was like for the youngest members of the cult, tales that were by turns horrifying and poignant, tales of beatings and sexual abuse. The children's accounts raised larger questions: Though their bruises have healed, what about the emotional toll? What kind of future awaits the children of the cult? Can they ever expect to lead normal lives?

The answer is, maybe. Unfortunately, therapists have had a surfeit of experience with children traumatized by war, inner-city life, family abuse and other present-day horrors. Typically such children suffer from flashbacks and nightmares for many years, reliving the early terror over and over again. And, without treatment, they may later repeat the abuse—this time as aggressors.

[2]Article by Ginny Carroll and Melinda Beck. From *Newsweek* 121:48–50 My 17 '93. Copyright © 1993 by Newsweek, Inc. Reprinted with permission.

After the initial shoot-out in February with federal agents, 21 youngsters, age 5 months to 12 years, were released to the custody of the Texas child-welfare agency. They were sent to the Methodist Home. There, psychiatrists and social workers helped them prepare for new lives; all but five children now live with relatives.

In their conversations with therapists, the youngest survivors described a twisted universe completely dominated by David Koresh. Former cult members corroborate much of what the children say. For the children, the ordinary now seems exotic. At the Methodist Home, one 3-year-old was transfixed by the magic of a flush toilet. He kept pushing the silvery lever, watching the water swirl down the bowl.

The children indicate that their life was, at best, spartan. They lived with their mothers in dormitory-like rooms decorated with colorful drawings and paper cutouts. But just below the surface, there was evil. According to ex-followers who have talked to the children, Koresh repeatedly committed statutory rape. He filled his sermons with graphic sexual talk. Corporal punishment was the rule; visitors to the ranch and ex-followers say the beatings lasted many minutes. Lonnie Little, a Michigan man, observed one such beating when he visited the compound in 1990 in an unsuccessful attempt to rescue his son Jeff, who died in the April 19 fire at the age of 32. When a young boy was "acting up," Koresh told his mother to "take care of that." According to Little, she complied immediately, beating her son with a stick for 15 minutes.

Such accounts played an important role in Attorney General Janet Reno's decision to inject tear gas into the compound on April 19. She cited concern about ongoing physical abuse of children as one of her main reasons for agreeing to the attack—although the FBI later backed off a bit. Much of her information came from FBI officials who had read a report prepared by Dr. Bruce Perry, a Baylor College of Medicine psychiatrist who worked with 19 of the children.

They had been indoctrinated to believe that there were only two kinds of people: good and evil, Perry says. All the righteous people were at Ranch Apocalypse; everyone else was bad. "The group was safe but under constant threat," says Perry. The paranoia was reinforced by the Feb. 28 shoot-out in which six cult members and four agents of the federal Bureau of Alcohol, Tobacco and Firearms were killed. To most children, that day would have been unmitigated horror—bullets flying, adults they loved lying dead and wounded while helicopters hovered nearby. To the cult children, it was the fulfillment of Koresh's prophecy.

In their world, weapons and violence were the norm. Scott Mabb, 11, and his brother, Jake, 9, who now live with their father in South Dakota, often talked about Koresh's arsenal. The boys said they used to watch Koresh fire a giant gun that stood on a tripod, and then retrieve the casings to earn privileges, like firing BB guns.

It took a while for the children to feel comfortable enough to talk about one of their big secrets: their belief that the standoff would end violently and that their parents would die. "The kids were quite smug about the concept that they knew what was going to happen and we didn't," says Perry. "They were under the presumption that everybody in there was going to die and that David was going to return from heaven and kill all the evil ones who had killed the members of their community, and then they'd all be reunited in heaven." At the Methodist Home, some of the children were excited when they saw a white van similar to one Koresh had driven. Officials made sure the van stayed away from the children after that.

Koresh's prophecies were his justification for the hardships inflicted on his followers and their children. In 1989, he declared that only he would be allowed to have sex with the female cult members, including mothers and young daughters. At 12, girls moved from the second-floor quarters they shared with their mothers to gender-segregated adult quarters. "It was an intrinsic part of his teachings that he would have sexual relations with young girls," says David Bunds, a former member. Bunds says that when Koresh took up with one girl, he "was having problems penetrating her, because she was so young and little. He told her to start using tampons, the kind that you insert in, to make herself larger."

At least five of the 17 children who died in the fire at the compound were believed to be Koresh's. Three were sired in liaisons with child brides; two others, Cyrus, 8, and Star, 6, were the products of Koresh's legal union with his wife, Rachel, 23, who also died. They married when she was 14.

To many girls, being chosen by Koresh was an honor they eagerly sought. Koresh "wouldn't do it unless you wanted it," says Jeannine Bunds, 51, who was one of Koresh's wives, along with her daughter, Robyn. "It wasn't about sex, but he was a very appealing, sexual person . . . He didn't say, 'Oooh, you've got sexy boobs.' He just loved the idea of womanhood . . . and he made you feel special." A union with Koresh was spiritual, says Robyn Bunds, who met Koresh when she was 14 and slept with him when she was 17. "You're going to marry this guy and he's God, and someday he will be resurrected as a perfect human being," says Bunds, now 23 and living in California. "He's perfect, and he's going to father your children. What more can you ask for?" In fact, Bunds says she was so committed to Koresh that she left in 1990, nine months after Koresh started sleeping with her mother, because she was tired of the abuse. Her son by Koresh, Shaun, is now 4.

Younger children, boys and girls, were exposed to explicit sexual material in Koresh's "sermons." Perry, the psychiatrist, has an audiotape of one Bible-study session where he says children were present. In it, Perry says, Koresh "talks about stripping off the clothes of a young girl and 'whacking' it to her right there." Lonnie Little heard similar sermons in 1990. On one occasion, Little says, Koresh "went on for about an hour and a half about the evils of masturbation. He used every gutter word and teenage word you could think of in front of this mixed group," which included young children.

At times Koresh did try to control his own sexual impulses toward children—and the impulses of other men in the cult. Several years ago Koresh decreed that no Branch Davidian man could change a girl baby's diapers because they might become aroused. Koresh was proud of this restriction. When child-welfare workers investigated allegations of child abuse last year, Koresh told them about the rule and his reasons for imposing it, according to Perry's report.

In his report, Perry says that all of the children exhibited a "permeating and pervasive fear of displeasing David or betraying his 'secrets'." However, the only evidence of physical abuse he and other child-welfare workers found were small circular bruises on the buttocks of several of the little girls.

Dick DeGuerin, the lawyer for Koresh's mother, contends that none of the activities at the ranch constitutes abuse, although he concedes that the Davidians had a lifestyle outside broadly accepted norms. "At what point does society have a right to step in and say you have to raise your family our way? It's applying Yuppie values to people who choose to live differently. These were loving families." He points out that Perry failed to find any physical evidence of sexual abuse, although the psychiatrist does say that the girls did not have gynecological exams.

Some of the children's more fantastic stories may not be true. In his report, Perry mentions that several children said dead babies were kept in the freezer until they could be buried or burned. Perry says that there's no way to determine the accuracy of these stories.

The next few months will be a crucial test of the children's ability to recover. "These children have many, many strengths," Perry says. "Everyone who worked with them liked them." They adjusted to David Koresh and Ranch Apocalypse. Can living in the outside world be any worse?

AN EMOTIONAL MOONSCAPE[3]

Suppose he was right. Suppose, after all, David Koresh was not just the half-crazed leader of a fringe religious sect but a genuine, board-certified Redeemer, come to prep the world for the Apocalypse. What if Koresh did have to take harsh repressive measures with his followers for their own good, to keep them from straying into the pagan world? And what if the federal forces arrayed against him really were malignant agents of the Devil, bent on gumming up his divine mission?

Looney as that gospel may have sounded to outsiders, scores of seemingly rational, intelligent adults on the inside believed it faithfully enough to follow its prophet into the fire. So what could be expected of 21 surviving children who spent most or all of their brief lives under Koresh's magnetic sway? For them, all is confusion. Released into the custody of Texas child authorities after the first deadly shoot-out at the Ranch Apocalypse compound, they have found themselves suddenly bereft of the parents, the teachers and the overarching authority figure who made the rules. Some wary and secretive, others clinging and anxious, these are kids not just orphaned but emptied of moral certitude. At the very least, says psychiatrist Bruce Perry, head of a team of volunteer counselors who've been treating them for the past two months, they will need "a whole new set of internal landmarks." That may be only part of the challenge therapists face in restoring

[3]Article by David Gelman. From *Newsweek* 121:52–54 My 17 '93. Copyright © 1993 by Newsweek, Inc. Reprinted with permission.

the Koresh kids to the real world—or rather, the world the rest of us live in.

Not that the doctors lack know-how. They have built substantial expertise on the traumatized young, based on studies of children in war zones from Mozambique to Chicago, as well as victims of natural disasters. Relatively little work has been done with young cult survivors, but in at least one respect the findings among all victimized children are similar. Most show signs of Posttraumatic Stress Disorder (PTSD), a syndrome marked by nightmares and psychic numbing, among other problems, that was reported mostly in Vietnam combat veterans. Reactions to extreme stress can vary with age and temperament. But some doctors estimate that at least 80 percent of the Branch Davidian children will experience PTSD. "There's been a major and horrific set of experiences for these children," says Saul Levine, head of child and adolescent psychiatry at the University of California, San Diego, in La Jolla. "Regardless of any therapy they get, this was for them a holocaust, one of the worst possible disasters. The chances that they are unscathed are very poor indeed. It's very common that they will have a bland, affectless response right now, only to be reminded years later in dreams, memories or psychopathology."

The psychopathology, in particular, worries doctors. A troubling pattern of repetition seems to play out in childhood trauma. As many as 70 percent of child abusers and wife beaters, for instance, turn out to have been abused children themselves. David Koresh, too, said he was abused. "So often the problem recurs because a person seeks a way of turning the passive-victim experience into the active mode of being a perpetrator," says UCLA child psychiatrist Dr. Spencer Eth. Does that mean some of the young Davidians will grow up to be oppressive parents? Not necessarily. Therapists try to find a healthier outlet for the active impulse, and sometimes they succeed.

For the Koresh kids, it is too early to say what the outcome will be. For one thing, there are still too many unanswered questions about what really happened to them in the cult. Indeed, the reports that emerged during the long siege of Ranch Apocalypse were as reductively black and white in their way as Koresh's teaching. Life inside "was not this horrible, bleak picture," acknowledges Perry, after his two-month examination of the children. Researchers have only been able to piece together a vague image of what the daily routine was like for the children, Perry says, but evidently not everything that went on was bad. "Many of the kids are very open about the fact that they really liked living there, and it was a nice place, and they felt happy and healthy." That, of course, wasn't the whole picture. Many also have recounted stories of harsh discipline, including physical punishments. And daily, the kids were being told that "the outside world was not good, that there were people out there who wanted to hurt them and would misunderstand them."

That probably accounts for the lingering secretiveness of many of the children. Therapists treating them in Waco's Methodist Home found them adept at dodging certain questions about life in the cult. "They use these pat comments or distraction techniques to get you away from really finding out the truth," says Perry. "We'd say, 'Well, you've heard people say David had all these wives. What do you think about that?' And they'd say something like, 'Read Psalm 53'." When the children first arrived at the Methodist Home, Perry notes, they set up a kind of miniature version of the Davidian social structure. An older male child and an older female child were said to have the "light," the state of grace that signified maturity in Koresh's eyes. "The boys sat with the boys and the girls sat with the girls, and they were exceptionally compliant." But as relatives came to claim various kin, this structure broke down and the children lapsed into more typical behavior.

The transition to living with family members again may be critical for these children. "They have trouble developing trusting relationships with adults," says Perry. "The most meaningful adults in their life are gone, including their biological parents. All those adults around whom you organize your development are gone." The Davidian blurring of lines between parental and other authority figures creates further problems.

Trust may be the key issue right now. Psychologists say that like adults, children often become cunning and manipulative in a repressive atmosphere. They develop stratagems to get things they want. In a new social system, they quickly begin wondering what the new rules are, what the people in charge are looking for. "Once they figure out they can't escape you," says Susan Andersen, an associate professor of psychology at New York University, "they'll try to figure out what they can do to manipulate you, to please you. I would think there's likely to be a lot of pretending involved." Therapists have to gain the child's trust by proving that they really care. At some point, perhaps to test the adult, the child might do something he's sure would bring punishment. A good therapist, says Andersen, will respond instead by showing understanding: "That will be the beginning of the child's realizing that it's safe to tell the truth."

Such an incident did occur at the Methodist Home, according to staff members. When one boy accidentally spilled milk—the kind of infraction that might have incurred a beating at Ranch Apocalypse—he cringed and instinctively raised his hand over his head. But a staff member quickly assured him he wasn't going to be struck. Above all, says Perry, therapists tried to be nonthreatening with the children—a policy that might well be practiced by any future caregivers. Staff members made it a point not to pry or ask too many questions. "The majority of it was completely nonintrusive. It was being with them, eating with them, playing with them. And when the kids would bring up a topic where they were upset, we had the staff literally right there who could provide nurturance."

It wasn't always easy to observe the no-threat rule. Jack Daniels, president of the Methodist Home, says the Davidian children at first were taught separately in their living quarters but then began attending classes outside the compound at the Methodist school. On the first day of class, one of the Davidians refused to relinquish the computer when his time was up. To discipline the boy, school officials decided he would be the last to use the computer the next day. When Daniels relayed that word to him, the boy launched into a rambling, flaky explanation about why he had needed to stay at the machine because of a game he was playing. Daniels told him that nevertheless he would be relegated to last in line. "He swelled up," says Daniels, "and said that in that case, he wasn't going to school. I said he had no choice, he was going. You could feel it in the air—he was just dying for me to make him do something. I raised my voice and repeated he would go to school. Then he decided he had to do it, but to maintain his defiance, he rolled off the sofa and rolled all the way down the hall to his room. It was a challenge to show him you could enforce discipline without physical contact or abuse."

The children, in fact, seem to have moved from one kind of conformist society to another. Only instead of just figuring out ways to manipulate the rules of their new milieu, they will have to adapt to them—a process that may be far from smooth. Perry is convinced there will be good outcomes for many of the children. All are still receiving some form of counseling and treatment—

and will continue to do so for the foreseeable future. Perry's team will also stay in contact with them for a time, to monitor their progress in adjusting to their new lives.

The adjustment may be rough going. Symptoms of post-traumatic stress can be immediate: in the first three weeks after their release, the Davidian children showed such typical signs as sleeplessness, hypervigilance, elevated heart rates. But other symptoms can turn up years later. Lenore Terr, a professor of psychiatry at the University of California, San Francisco, studied 25 children kidnapped aboard their school bus and buried under-ground in a truck trailer for 16 hours, in a bizarre incident near Chowchilla, Calif. Four years after the event, Terr found that "every child exhibited posttraumatic effects," including repeated nightmares, feelings of shame and, particularly disturbing in people so young, a "severe pessimism" about their lives. Having narrowly escaped death, most of them doubted they would live long; some died in their dreams.

It's not unusual for people to feel shame about a set of circum-stances in which they were the victims. In subtle—or sometimes not so subtle—ways, they are made to feel responsible for their own misfortune, the classic case being the rape victim. Former cultists seem to carry a particular stigma when they've been sexu-ally abused. Clinical psychologist Margaret Thaler Singer, of the University of California, Berkeley, has treated hundreds of ex-cultists. She considers it a kind of "intellectual mistake" to equate sexual abuse in outside society with sexual abuse in cults. "They're two different programs, so to speak," she says. In outside society, because of the furtiveness and guilt attached to the act, an abused child is made to feel "part of an illicit, dirty conspiracy." In the cults, the abuse tends to be more open, an accepted if not ap-proved part of the group's behavior. "Children may resent it, they may hate it, but they see it happen to other children and they don't feel they're the only one—which is such an important as-pect of the way it's experienced on the outside." And, Singer adds, she has interviewed scores of abused former cultists who grew up to be well-functioning adults.

Other psychologists agree that the readjustment victims make can hinge on how outside society receives them. After studying children in war zones around the world, James Garbarino, presi-dent of Chicago's Erikson Institute, concludes that their experi-ence was not unlike what happened at Waco. In Mozambique and Cambodia, he says, he and his team of researchers encountered apocalyptic events and children subjected to strange rituals. In Mozambique, children kidnapped into the opposition army group, Renamo, were sometimes subjected to "heinous" punishments and forced to serve as executioners. How the children handled the stress and guilt afterward was partly a matter of individual differences of temperament. But a lot depended also on reintegrating them into the community. Many of the children came home originally as prisoners of war, having served in the enemy army. But community activists persuaded friends and neighbors to welcome them back. "It took a lot of effort to do that," says Garbarino, "and to get the kids to give up the idea they were responsible for the bad things that happened." By the same token, he says, what some of the Davidian kids will have to face is that both in their own minds and in the minds of those around them, their identity may be tied up with Koresh. "So it's much more than a set of narrow psychiatric symptoms. It's more a philosophical and community problem of what kind of identity the child has," Garbarino concludes.

By now, according to Perry, some of the children have formed "very intense attachments" to staff members who have worked with them over the past two months. Under the circumstances, he thinks that their behavior is normal and predictable. "What's going on is that these kids are clinging to anybody who is available to kind of nurture and take care of them." Obviously, he adds, those attachments will have to be gradually pried loose and transferred to the families that have begun getting custody of the children.

Whoever takes over the care and welfare of the Waco waifs will be hard pressed to replace what they have already lost. Only 10 children were left at the Methodist Home when the Branch Davidian compound burned to the ground. Perry says that when the children were told of the fire they reacted "pretty much as you'd expect from any other group of children who were told that their loved ones were dead. There was some disbelief, sadness, anger, confusion and outright fear about what the future held."

For all they've been through, the future may not hold any comparable ordeals for the cult children. Some of them seem likely to become productive members of society; some no doubt will continue to bear the emotional scars of their experiences for years to come. For qualified observers such as psychiatrist Levine, "the psychological jury is still out." Levine cites a study by the Ford Foundation in the 1970s of hundreds of children in different family situations. Long-term outcomes showed no significant differences, as long as there was even a "modicum" of such things as loving, setting of rules and teaching. If those things are done it doesn't really matter what the social setting is, Levine says. "If not, then these Davidian kids are in jeopardy." But of course, the jeopardy was there from the time their parents sought the false comfort of a cult.

IV. CULTS AND CONTROVERSY

EDITOR'S INTRODUCTION

Jim Jones's People's Temple and David Koresh's Branch Dividians may have attracted the most attention, but that should not obscure the fact that scores of other marginal religious groups exist in America today. These groups are not as anomalous as they might seem. In the nineteenth century a large number of idiosyncratic religious movements were born. Christian Science and Mormonism, to give only two examples, came into being at that time and were among the most controversial "cults" of their era.

Section four of this volume begins with an appendix from J. Gordon Melton's informative survey of modern alternative religions, *The Cult Experience*. He notes that more than 600 alternative religions are practiced in the U.S. and Canada, and that 75 of them may be classified as cults. Among others, he comments on The Church of Armageddon, The Church of Scientology, The International Society of Krisha Consciousness (Hare Krishna) and The Unification Church. Of these, Melton describes the Unification Church and the Church of Scientology as the most controversial. Melton's survey is followed by Elizabeth Gleick's and Pam Lambert's profile of some current cult figures. Writing in *People Weekly,* they portray Keith Ham, a key figure in the Hare Krishna movement but who was expelled by its governing board and is presently appealing a 1991 conviction in federal court for authorizing beatings, kidnapping, and murder.

Scandal and controversy have always followed marginal religions, as Elizabeth Nordbeck notes in *U.S.A. Today* magazine. Not only is there a cult movement but also an Anti-Cult movement, made up of such groups as the American Family Foundation and the Cult Awareness Network (CAN). Viewing religious communes as a threat that ensnare young people and wean them away from their families and friends, the anti-cultists attempt to get individuals back, and "deprogram" them. Nordbeck points out that many myths about cults i.e., recruits are invariably brainwashed and are never free to leave of their own accord. In her article, she asks for balanced judgment in regard to these churches. In *The Nation,* Alexander Cockburn faults the ATF and FBI for their handling of the Branch Davidian crisis, arguing that they relied too much on the advice of cult haters. Cockburn points out that Rick Ross, a cult "hunter" with a "history of emotional disturbance," was also one of the government's principal consultants for the Waco siege. The final article in this section, by Charles L. Harper and Bryan L. Le Beau in the journal *Sociology of Religion,* traces the movement of controversial religions toward eventual acceptability within the cultural establishment. They remark that Christianity itself was once regarded as a "dangerous" cult.

A BRIEF GUIDE TO THE MAJOR ALTERNATIVE RELIGIONS[1]

More than 600 religious groups in the United States and in Canada could properly be termed alternative religions. Most are so small that the likelihood of meeting a member is slight. Others have made homes for themselves on the religious landscape and could almost be considered accepted; Christian Science is such a group. Many alternative religions serve particular ethnic groups and are not seen by people outside these ethnic communities.

Of the 600 groups, approximately 75 have been identified as cults by modern anti-cultists. These groups are identified mainly by their reception of a large percentage of their members from among the young white, middle-class population of the 1970s. Many are in their first generation of existence in North America. The largest of these groups number less than 10,000, and the two most famous—the Hare Krishna and the Unification Church— number less than 5,000. On the average these groups have 1,000 to 3,000 members. Thus, an estimated 150,000 individuals are involved in the so-called cults at any one time. Each of these groups experiences a large overturn in membership.

Reports of cults numbering in the thousands and involving

[1]Article by J. Gordon Melton. From appendix A of *The Cult Experience.* Copyright © 1982 by The Pilgrim Press. Reprinted with permission of The Pilgrim Press, Cleveland, Ohio.

people in the millions contain grossly exaggerated figures circulated by anti-cult groups to promote a climate of hysteria. Such
figures have no basis in fact and represent, at best, the wild speculations of those who make their living fighting alternative religions.

Of the 75 cults, almost all attention has been focused on 13
alternative religions:
The Church of Armageddon
The Church Universal and Triumphant
The Church of Scientology
The International Society for Krishna Consciousness (Hare
Krishna)
Transcendental Meditation
Divine Light Mission
Zen Buddhism
Nichiren Shoshu of America (Soka Gakkai)
The Children of God/Family of Love
The Christian Foundation
The Local Church
Way International
The Unification Church
Besides these thirteen groups we have added consideration of two
groups rarely encountered by anti-cultists but which nevertheless
have made an impact on the cult problem because of the general
cultural fear of them—Witchcraft and Satanism. These groups
are discussed under five headings: communal, psychic, magical,
eastern, and Christian.

This guide attempts to introduce each group through its history and teachings, with the goal of providing a start at understanding the group's peculiarities. Where possible, a further
source for more in-depth study is cited. Often this source is a
publication distributed by the group or one authored by a sympa-
thetic outsider. One should encounter the group on its own terms
before formulating a criticism. We also note that most books written about cults are hostile to the groups and highly inaccurate in
reporting their beliefs and practices. Such books are more interested in refuting the groups than in giving readers any understanding of them.

All the great religious traditions have made a place for people
who wish to live a strong communal existence built on the mutual
sharing and consumption of the individual's resources. Many religious groups, including Christianity, were founded as communal

groups. The Christian ideal of communal living spelled out in the book of Acts has continually inspired groups in the West during the past 2,000 years. Many of the communal groups that survive into a second generation abandon communal living. The Mormons, originally organized into the United Society, abandoned communal living in the 1840s and have since been plagued by schismatic groups that wish to reinstitute what they consider an essential of Mormon faith.

America has had two main periods in which numerous communes were formed. The first occurred in the 1840s; the second in the 1960s. Successful communes, a small minority of the whole, survive the first winter and continue for many years; a few survive into the second and third generations. Those that survive do so because of a strong organization that can stave off the continual lure of the world to abandon their peculiar ways. Thus, the successful commune generally has a strong (often autocratic) leadership and a strong ethos—usually a particular religion— that serve both to separate the group from the world and to bind the members of the group closely together. Too much interaction with nonmembers, especially with persons to whom members might have emotional ties, is highly destructive of communal existence. Communal groups adopt mechanisms to prevent illicit intercourse with the world. They change their names, develop in-group jargon and rituals, and hold secrets. Commonly included in their private world are practices that have a clear logic and/or rationale within the context but which, when looked on by an outsider, can appear sinister, psychotic, or just plain weird.

Sex is a powerful force that, if uncontrolled, can destroy a communal group quickly. Communal groups usually adopt one of two patterns: abstinence or group marriage. In the former, a pattern of the Hare Krishna, sexual feelings are sublimated and directed to communal symbols; in the Hare Krishna's case, the deities. Other groups—the Oneida Community being the most famous—adopt a pattern in which sexual activity is diffused through the community; thus no particular infatuation can replace the group as the first concern of any individual.

The Church of Armageddon

This group became famous when a major network filmed an attempted deprogramming by Ted Patrick of one of its members. Then the press discovered that Steve Allen's son was a leading member. The Church was founded in 1969 by Paul Erdmann in Seattle, Washington.

The communal organization of the Church of Armageddon takes the form of an extended family, and each member takes the family name Israel. As a first name they take the name of a virtue or attribute—love, serious, contemplation, etc. Paul Erdmann, the leader, is known as Love Israel, and the group is frequently referred to as the Love Israel Family.

On joining, members give up their earthly goods to the group and renounce the world. In particular, they renounce the worldly traditions of matrimony. As with Christian monastics, they see themselves both collectively and individually as married to Christ. Members also see themselves as married to one another, with the men as husbands having authority over the women as wives. In practice, their relationship is as brothers and sisters. The leaders of the Church have the authority to allow individual "bonding" for the purpose of having children.

A book written by Love Israel entitled *Love* serves as the standard of teaching for the group. The Church of Armageddon is the continuation of Israel (Old Testament) and follows the primitive teachings of Jesus Christ (New Testament). Eating and drinking are sacramental; whatever is eaten is the body of Christ, and whatever is drunk, his blood. When one joins he or she is freed from the past life in the world of sin and death. Baptism by immersion is practiced.

Headquarters of the Church is in a residential section of Seattle. Outposts of the community in Hawaii and Alaska were recently closed. There are approximately 400 members.

The Church has been accused of violent activity, but as yet no evidence of such activity has been presented. Much of the substance of the accusation derived from the death in 1972 of two members who took an overdose of toluene, a solvent that alters the state of consciousness when inhaled and that was used in a religious rite. This group was also accused of trying to take over Queen Anne Hill, the section of Seattle its original commune is located in, but time has proved the charge to be empty speculation. Members live a clannish existence and have cut themselves off from many worldly pursuits.

Psychic Groups

During the 20th century the development of parapsychology into a widely recognized scientific endeavor has encouraged the growth of many groups that base their beliefs around psychic-occult phenomena. Such groups, including the Spiritualists and Theosophists, were among the original groups labeled cults early in this century. Spiritualism and Theosophy have been around for more than a century and have a membership that reflects their maturity. Although neither benefited greatly from the influx of young adults into alternative religions in the 1970s, some basic understanding of each will help in understanding one of the major groups labeled cult—the Church Universal and Triumphant.

A basic belief of Spiritualism is that certain people, called mediums, can through trance or just clear psychic perception contact entities of the spirit world. In classic Spiritualism the primary entities mediums attempted to contact were the recently deceased relatives of persons who attended the seances—meetings whose purpose was spirit contact. Spiritualists believed that, along with the dead, they frequently contacted other entities, highly evolved spirits, from whom they could learn of the true nature of life and of the life to come. Out of classic Spiritualism arose a form of teaching Spiritualism in which the major activity consisted of learning about spiritual life from spirit teachers.

Theosophy grew out of Spiritualism. Madame Helena Petrovna Blavatsky, Theosophy's main teacher and leader, claimed contact with a series of evolved beings, whom she called mahatmas or masters. Some of these beings were spirits; some were reincarnated in bodies. Together, the masters formed a spiritual hierarchy between humans and the divine, with Madame Blavatsky as their spokesperson. The hierarchy governed the world and controlled the various spheres of human existence.

Closest to humanity and in direct contact with Madame Blavatsky were the Lords of the Seven Rays. In occult terms the basic areas of human life, such as beauty, science, devotion, and service, were associated with the seven colors of the light spectrum. Light itself is, of course, the most characteristic manifestation of the divine. When light comes to a person this person intuitively perceives truth. When a particularly colored light comes to someone he or she perceives the truth in one area of existence.

During her life Madame Blavatsky was the main person in contact with the masters. After her death the leaders of the Theosophical Society frowned on anyone who attempted to replace her as the regular go-between with the masters. Some who tried, such as Alice Bailey, were eased out of the group.

Among those who claimed to have come in contact with the masters, Guy Ballard (AKA Godfre Ray King) established his own competing group—the Great I AM—in Chicago in the 1930s. After his death, during World War II, his wife succeeded him and led the group until her death, in the late 1970s.

Over the past several decades the I AM splintered into a number of groups—The Bridge to Freedom, the Ascended Master Fellowship, and the Sanctuary of the Master's Presence. Of these various splinters the only one to attain anything similar to the success of the original I AM group has been the Summit Lighthouse, better known by the name it adopted in the 1970s: the Church Universal and Triumphant.

The Church Universal and Triumphant

The Church Universal and Triumphant was founded as the Summit Lighthouse in 1958 by Mark and Elizabeth Clare Prophet, two former members of the Bridge to Freedom, the original I AM splinter. For many years the group was headquartered in Colorado Springs but moved to Pasadena in the midseventies, after Mark's death in 1973, and then to its present location near Malibu, California, site of a former Roman Catholic college. During the 1970s the present name gradually replaced the original one.

The Church has a sophisticated theology drawn from Theosophy and centered on the Prophets' roles as communication links with the Ascended Masters. Since his death Mark has been considered one of the Lords of the Seven Rays. At present Elizabeth Prophet is the special messenger of the spiritual hierarchy, especially of one master, El Morya. During many of the gatherings at which Ms. Prophet presides a communication from one or more of the masters to those gathered is the main event.

The Church also follows the practice of decreeing, a form of spiritual exercise developed by Guy Ballard. Decrees are short statements of one's wishes for the self or the world stated in such a way that the words demand the divine to act on these wishes. Such decrees are repeated in a loud voice and a chanting rhythm.

During the 1970s a distinct change took place in the Church. In its early years the Summit Lighthouse related to members primarily through the mail. Members received periodicals and lessons from the Colorado Springs headquarters and gathered in the summer for conferences. In the late 1970s Ms. Prophet, now styled as Guru Ma, borrowed an image from many of the Eastern teachers, began to evangelize among young adults and to build groups of followers, congregations, around the country. To further expand its outreach to the public the Church increased the number of books and written materials it produced and created several sets of tapes.

During the several decades of its existence, primarily through its mail courses, the Church has built a large following, numbering in the thousands in the United States and with an additional significant following in West Africa (Ghana and Liberia).

The main criticism of the Church Universal and Triumphant, besides the usual brainwashing claims, derives from the group's manifest prosperity, as evidenced, for example, by the purchase of the college campus in California (renamed Camelot), the slick publications, and the tuition charges at Summit University (the Church's school). Although the figures may seem large and like any sizable religious organization the Church has a large cash flow, no evidence of improper use or accumulation of money has been presented, even though several high-level members of the group have left it.

(Most accusations against religious organizations for having a money orientation or a great deal of wealth are made apart from any analysis of what happens to the money a religious group takes in, how this money compares to the money taken in by more established churches and synagogues, and how much money it takes to operate a religious institution, such as a school. Apart from such comparable figures, reflections on a particular group's high cash flow hides an unstated and unproven accusation that the leader(s) are hoarding the wealth and getting rich at the expense of gullible followers.

The accusation of a religion's existing only to accumulate money for the benefit of a few is as old as religion itself. And on occasion religion has been undeniably so used. But apart from evidence that, in fact, a few are growing wealthy from the givings of the members, claims—covert or overt—based merely on the calculated cash flow of a group become empty. Evidence that a few are growing wealthy would be grounds for the removal of their tax exempt status by the Internal Revenue Service.)

The Church of Scientology

The Church of Scientology was founded in 1955 by L. Ron Hubbard. During his earlier years Hubbard served as an officer in the U.S. Navy, operated as an investigator for the Los Angeles Police Department, authored fiction and nonfiction books, and became an accomplished amateur philosopher. His philosophical and theological speculations led to his development of a practical system for human improvement, which he termed Dianetics. Scientology is the natural extension of Dianetics into a total philosophical and theological teaching and program.

The Church's belief is quite eclectic. Hubbard draws ideas from both Eastern and Ancient Greek thought as well as from modern occultism and individualism. The Church teaches that humans are basically good and ever strive to survive. Each person is designated a Thetan, i.e., a soul, an individual force. The Thetan controls the body and is the essence of the responsible self. The incarnated Thetan is hindered from full ability to express goodness and survive by painful past experiences. The attainment of self-knowledge allows the individual to increase his or her ability to survive and express the good innate within the self.

The Church's activities all aim at increasing self-knowledge. The Scientologist begins his or her work on the mind, which has stored all experiences, including mental image pictures of past experiences of pain and negativity (engrams). Engrams are kept in what is called the Reactive mind. When unconsciously released they impose themselves on the person. When consciously released they can be erased and denied their power.

A special pastoral counseling process called auditing is used to assist individuals to remove engrams. Once clear, the Scientologist can begin to develop the potentials of the Thetan, which includes the ability to free itself from the body for short periods.

No church has been involved in so much controversy as has the Church of Scientology, with the possible exception of the Unification Church. It has since its founding been almost continuously in court on a variety of issues ranging from suing the Food and Drug Administration to defending itself against charges of stealing from the government. It took to task for libel authors who wrote about the Church, and it usually won. For more than a decade it has battled with the Internal Revenue Service for its tax exemption.

Of all the religious groups in America the Church of Scientology is the most difficult to evaluate. It has made enemies who will go far out of their way—and have—to see it destroyed. It fights just as tenaciously to defend itself at all costs. For more than 20 years it has been involved in a growing war with the anti-cult movement and the government. So complex has this situation become that only when the dust settles from the various court cases still in progress will a full understanding be possible.

Certain facts lead one to tentative conclusions. First, the conviction of Scientology leaders in the recent case of theft of government property has demonstrated that overzealous Scientologists have gone to great extremes—even to the point of committing a felony—to defend the Church. The same case also proved that the Church has been continually lied to by government agencies. The release of reams of secret Scientology files, while containing some evidence of highly questionable behavior on the Church's part—such as the collection of dossiers on Church "enemies"—also failed to reveal that the Church was engaged in widespread nefarious plots.

Interestingly, the controversies in which this church has been involved have all centered on the Guardian's Office, a special division of the Church set up to defend the Church against what it felt were unjustified attacks and slander. While the rest of the Church carried out its program, individuals in the Guardian's Office had a great deal of freedom to carry out actions they felt were necessary to defend the Church against its enemies. In 1981 the Church announced a wholesale replacement of leaders in this office.

Thus, the final word on the Church of Scientology must wait. Meanwhile, the Church has remained most open to inquiries by interested individuals who wish to know the Church's position on the many charges that have been leveled against it.

Magical Groups

Few words in the cult realms stir emotions as much as Witchcraft and Satanism. The two have been locked together at least since the Middle Ages, and both began a comeback in the 1960s. Although neither has received the attention of anti-cultists that some of the more public groups have, in the interface between parents and sons and daughters involved in an alternative religion, Witchcraft is more likely to appear than any group in this guide. There are approximately 30,000 to 40,000 Witches and Neo-Pagans, collectively three times as many participants as the most successful of the better known cults.

To understand Witchcraft and Satanism it is necessary to distinguish them. Whatever might have been their connection in centuries past, today they are distinct phenomena. Satanism is the worship of the Christian personification of evil. Even though it is a rare phenomenon, it has been known periodically to make an appearance in Western culture. Witchcraft, at least as practiced today, is a revival of ancient pagan fertility religion believed by its adherents to have been the dominant pre-Christian religion of Europe. Its main deities are the Great Mother Goddess and the Horned God—Diana and Pan—derived from Greek mythology. Although there are many thousands of Neo-Pagans, there have never been more than 2,000 or 3,000 Satanists and that was in the early seventies, at the height of the popularity of Anton LeVey's Church of Satan.

Thus, to interact correctly in a situation where one party is self-identified as a Witch, it is important for all concerned to dismiss notions that the Witch is involved in bloody rituals, rites parodying Christian worship, and malevolent magic.

Witchcraft

Witchcraft, as practiced today, began in England in the 1940s. It was created (or revived) by Gerald Gardner, a retired British civil servant. While serving in southern Asia he had become attracted to magic and to the worship of the Mother Goddess. Once back in England he formed a coven, the basic organizational grouping in the Craft, and promulgated his teachings. He wrote a set of rituals that have become widely circulated, and following Gardner's lead others produced materials also.

After Gardner's books were published, in the 1950s, people flocked to him for initiation into Witchcraft, and almost all present-day Neo-Pagan groups derive from his efforts. In the mid-1960s, several Americans—including Ray and Rosemary Buckland, and Donna Cole—traveled to England and brought back Gardner's teaching.

Witchcraft has two foci—magic and the Goddess. Magic is the art of causing change by an act of the will, using cosmic magical power. Witches use magical power mainly for high magic, changing the individual self into a perfected human. It can also be used for low, or mundane magic, making change in the visible world. The major uses are to heal and to assist a member of the coven to attain something, such as a new job. A moral principle, the Wiccan Rede—"Except ye harm none, do what thou wilt"—controls the use of magic, and except on rare occasions, curses against someone would not be used.

Witches worship the Earth Mother, although they call Her by many names, depending on which ancient form of Pagan thought attracts them. The setting of the Mother Goddess and the Horned God as the leading deities of Witchcraft sets Witches in search of a balanced life. They seek balance between inner-outer, male-female, passive-aggressive, and spiritual-material.

Witches are organized into small groups (usually five to fifteen people) called covens, although some Neo-Pagan groups call them groves or nests. These are autonomous groups that normally gather biweekly, on the full and new moons (esbats), and annually on eight major festivals (called sabbats). Worship is conducted inside a circle, the visible sign of a sphere imagined to surround the coven when it meets. In the basic ritual act, called "drawing down the moon," psychic energy is pictured as being raised in a cone over the coven and then pulled into the circle.

Witches do not recruit, and new members have to be self-motivated enough either to find a group or locate the books necessary to start a group of their own. Within the movement are a number of "solitaries," who work the Craft as a personal spiritual path without the more elaborate rituals of the group.

Satanism

Satanism, the worship of the Christian personification of evil, was revived in the mid-1960s by Anton LeVey, who founded the Church of Satan on April 30, 1966. For the Church, Satan is identified as Lucifer, the light-bearer, the principle of nature at its highest. Satan is also identified with the snake in the Garden of Eden, who destroyed innocence by bringing knowledge.

Satanists see themselves as developing the self to the fullest and upholding personal values as opposed to altruistic virtues. Because the self is the highest embodiment of life it is sacred, and indulgence and vital existence are proper modes of being.

As spread in the 1970s, Satanism manifested itself basically as a movement teaching self-assertion. It was not involved in animal sacrifice or acts of violence against individuals. These rare actions can be found as part of informal groups where psychopathology is present.

Because of the very nature of Satanism—either in its tamer aspect in teaching self-assertion or its more pathological one—it is a short-lived phenomenon and rarely involves individuals for more than a few years.

Eastern Groups

Eastern religion has been present in the United States since
the late 19th century but until the mid-1960s was largely confined
to Asian-American communities, intellectuals, and a few social-
ites. Then, in 1965, the Oriental Exclusion Acts were repealed,
and large-scale immigration began from India and was revived
from Japan. Along with the immigrants came religious leaders—
gurus (teachers) and swamis (monks). While making good newspaper copy because their dress and behavior differ from that of
Western priests and preachers, in Eastern society they occupy the
same positions as do the religious functionaries that are more
familiar to Americans. They come as both religious leaders of
immigrant communities and as missionaries of Eastern religions.

Within Eastern religion the basic leader is a guru, or sensei
(literally: teacher). Typically, the guru teaches the student (chela)
a set of spiritual techniques, which the student practices to attain
spiritual goals. The guru is also seen as an embodiment of the
spiritual goals and attainment of them is the source of the guru's
authority. Thus, an accomplished yogi has the authority to teach
yoga. The techniques of spiritual discipline vary widely. Yoga, for
example, may take the form of hatha (postures), karma (work),
bhakti (devotion), japa (repeating mantras), raja (meditation), or
tantra (sex). Meditation is the most popular spiritual discipline,
but among different groups the form of meditation varies tre-
mendously.

Almost all the Eastern groups currently functioning in the
United States were founded by a single teacher, who gathered a
small group of disciples around him and then spread as opportunity allowed. Following Eastern patterns, all spiritual authority
is invested in the guru, who passes it on to others as the group
requires. When a leader dies, this person is succeeded by someone previously appointed to be the leader's successor, a new leader elected by the group in some way, or a collective leadership.
Also, as the group grows and spreads into a national movement, it
must shift from reliance on personal contact with and instruction
from the leader and place increased reliance on more impersonal
methods of contact through printed instructional materials.

The basic problem of alternative religion—how to integrate
new members—is most obvious in the Eastern religions. Because
the average convert knows little of Eastern religion the new member must be put through a concentrated educational process dur-

ing the first few years of membership. This process, which takes the place of the learning a person raised in a Hindu or Buddhist society would normally receive during the childhood and teen years, is so intense because instead of just learning a few differences, as when a Methodist becomes a Presbyterian, the average new member must learn a whole new way to be religious.

International Society for Krishna Consciousness (Hare Krishna)

Second only to the Unification Church as a focus of the cult controversy, the Hare Krishna movement was founded in 1965 by A. C. Bhaktivedanta Swami Prabhupada, an independent teacher out of the Chaitanya tradition of Bengal. Lord Chaitanya Mahaprabhu (1486–1534), a contemporary of Martin Luther, led a bhaktiyoga reform movement within 16th-century Hinduism.

The Society takes its teachings from the *Bhagavad Gita*, one of several sacred Hindu books, and worships Krishna as the eternal, omniscient, omnipresent, omnipotent, and all-attractive Personality of Godhead. All actions are performed as acts of devotion to Krishna; for example, all food is offered to Krishna before it is eaten.

The main act of devotion is the repetition of the Hare Krishna mantra. The chanting of the words

Hare Krishna, Hare Krishna
Hare Hare Krishna Krishna
Hare Rama, Hare Rama
Hare Hare Rama Rama

is seen as the best method in this day and age of receiving the pure consciousness of God (in his incarnations of Krishna and Rama) and dispelling the maya (illusion) in which we are all immersed. The Society promotes the frequent recital of the mantra among its members as well as people in general.

The movement is organized on a noncloistered monastic model. Partly because of the demands of its ascetic life-style, the Society has not grown beyond a few thousand members, who rise early each day and follow a scheduled routine. A typical day includes a ritual bath, the marking of the body with clay (telok), service to the deity statues, public chanting of the Hare Krishna mantra (kirtan), and study of the Gita and related materials.

Because of the demands of the life of a Krishna member, devotees do little recruiting. Most new members are people who have heard of the movement and who come to a temple and ask to join. Usually they are either familiar with and inclined toward Eastern religion and/or are vegetarians. They are then put through a period of training to test their resolve and acceptability.

The main source of tension between Krishna devotees and their critics derives from the purity code. Devotees attempt to separate themselves from the world of illusion. They symbolize this separation by taking a ritual bath daily, abstaining from regular company with non-Krishnas, eating only prasadam (food offered to Krishna), taking a new name, and avoiding the reading of too many non-Krishna books. Avoiding contact with non-Krishnas can take the form of a devotee losing contact with his or her immediate family.

Krishnas have received negative criticism for their fund-raising in airports and other public facilities, and steps have been taken to limit their contact with passengers. Recently, wide media coverage was given to accusations that Krishnas were stockpiling weapons, after several weapons had been found in a member's automobile. Unfortunately, little coverage was given to a later announcement that no substance to the charge was discovered and that the Society, which is pacifist as a matter of basic teaching, had previously instructed the said member to get rid of his weapons. Although new members are still taken in, growth of the Society has slowed, and membership seems to have leveled out at around 3,000. Where temples are located a large group of non-members may gather on Sundays, when the Krishnas give their free feasts.

Transcendental Meditation

Transcendental Meditation (TM) is a yoga discipline featured in the teachings of an organization called the World Plan Executive Council. The corporate name refers to the plan for spreading the teachings of Maharishi Mahesh Yogi, its guru. The Maharishi came out of 13 years of seclusion with his teacher, Guru Dev, in 1958 and began spreading his teachings, with gained early notoriety when the Beatles, Mia Farrow, and Jane Fonda became TM practitioners.

The Council consists of five task-oriented structures. The International Meditation Society is the main structure to introduce TM to the general public. The Student International Meditation Society introduces TM to the student population. Maharishi International University is a regular four-year university that offers both bachelor's and master's degrees. The university, formerly Parson's College in Fairfield, Iowa, has shaped its curriculum on TM principles. The American Foundation for the Science of Creative Intelligence is working to introduce TM principles into the business community. Finally, the Spiritual Regeneration Movement works with the older generation, i.e., those over 30.

TM is a form of japa-yoga—meditation with a mantra. Unlike the Hare Krishna practice, the usual TM mantra consists of one or two words that are repeated silently and on which the meditator concentrates. The practice of TM allows the practitioner to contact the absolute field of pure being—unmanifested and transcendental. This being is the ultimate reality of creation. Once meditation begins, the individual also begins to "live the being," and the Maharishi offers instruction on correct thinking, speaking, action, behavior and health. The goal is God-realization. The Maharishi's teaching is the summation of the practical wisdom of the integrated life as advanced by the Vedic Rishis of Ancient India; that is, TM proposes to reach the spiritual goals of humanity in this generation.

TM had a spectacular growth during the 1970s. Almost a million people took the basic TM course, then, at the end of the decade, the number of new meditators dropped markedly and the organization suffered some dramatic reverses, occasioned partly by its unique position on the question of religion.

Hindus frequently claim that Hinduism is religion itself, whereas other religions are merely limited expressions of religion, i.e., a religion. TM has gone one step farther and declared itself not a religion. It states that TM is a technique that both the religious and the nonreligious can practice. The teachings are not theology, but the science of creative intelligence. Before the court decided in 1978 that, according to American legal usage, TM constituted a religion, the practice had penetrated many public institutions, and TM instructors were being supported by schools and the armed forces. This court decision constituted a major reversal for the World Plan Executive Council.

Then the Council announced that they had successfully taught TM practitioners to levitate. The Maharishi was immediately attacked by other Hindu teachers for misrepresenting Yoga. The press called on him to put up or shut up. In both instances his credibility was severely questioned. The growth of the seventies has slowed markedly, but TM centers can still be found in most U.S. cities.

Divine Light Mission

The Divine Light Mission was founded in India in 1960 by Sri Hans Ji Maharaj, a former member of the Radhasoami Satsang Beas. The Radhasoami is one of several neo-Sikh groups, each of which is headed by a leader considered by the members to be a perfect master, or satguru. The satguru's task is to teach members the path back to God and actively to lead them as they follow the path. Soon after founding the Mission, Sri Hans Ji died and was succeeded by his youngest son, then only eight years old. At the funeral, the son is reported to have addressed the assembled crowd, "Oh, you have been illusioned by maya (the delusion that suffering is real). Maharaj Ji is here, very much present amidst you. Recognize him, adore him, and obey him."

According to the tradition of the Mission, the young guru had been an unusual child, who began meditating at age two and was giving discourses to disciples at age six. In 1970, four years after taking leadership of the Mission, Guru Maharaj Ji proclaimed the dawn of a new era and began the international expansion that brought him to the United States the next year.

Maharaj Ji initiates followers (called premies, i.e., lovers of God) through the giving of knowledge. This process involves the instruction in four yoga techniques, which the premies practice daily as a means to realize their goals of spiritual enlightenment. The first technique involves the placing of the knuckles on the eyes, an action that produces flashes of light in the head (by producing pressure on the optic nerve). The second involves the plugging of the ears and concentrating on the inner sounds. The third involves concentrating on the sound of one's own breathing. Finally, the "nectar" is a technique in which the tongue is curled backward against the roof of the mouth.

The Divine Light Mission grew quickly in the early seventies but suffered a severe setback in 1973, when a large, expensive event in the Houston Astrodome proved a major disaster, financially and otherwise. In the late seventies the Mission became a low-key organization and stopped its attempts at mass appeal. Recently, Maharaj Ji quietly moved to Miami. The Mission has reportedly initiated over 50,000 people, but only a few thousand remain in the chain of ashrams that now dot the nation.

Buddhism began its spread from ethnic confines several decades before Hinduism partly because of the encounter of American soldiers with Japanese Buddhism during the occupation after

World War II. The first form of Buddhism to attract attention, Zen Buddhism became an integral part of the Beat Generation in the early 1950s.

Zen is a mystical form of Buddhism that stands in relation to Buddhism as a whole much as contemplative Catholicism does to Christianity. It was begun by Bodhidharma (d. 534) and has been passed along through a lineage of "enlightened" Zen masters. Along the way Zen divided into two major schools: Rinzai and Soto. Rinzai Zen uses a practice called the koan, which is an anecdotal event or utterance given to a student as a problem. Mastering the koan is seen as a means of enlightenment. Pure Soto Zen does not use the koan.

Both Rinzai Zen and Soto Zen use the typical Zen method of meditation—*zazen,* sitting meditation. Detailed instructions for zazen include positioning of the body, including the tongue and teeth. The eyes are kept open, in contrast to many meditation techniques. The goal of zazen is satori, mystical enlightenment.

Since Zen arrived, in 1893, and spread after World War II it has become the most popular form of Buddhism for non-Asiatic Americans. Presently, Zen centers can be found in most American cities, with a few—such as the Zen Meditation Center of Rochester (NY) and the Zen Center of San Francisco—heading up a chain of centers.

Soka Gakkai

Soka Gakkai is the popular name for Nichiren Shoshu, originally a lay movement that grew up among the Japanese followers of Nichiren Buddhism. Intensely nationalistic, it was suppressed by the Shinto government but revived after World War II. It went from less than a hundred members to approximately a quarter million.

Soka Gakkai became an object of strong dislike for most Japanese Buddhists and was even alienated from other Nichiren Buddhists, because it entered into politics and developed harsh proselytizing techniques. It organized its own political party, the Komei Kai, which in the 1960s became a major force on the national political scene.

The Nichiren Shoshu also engaged in a practice called shakubuku, literally translated "bend and flatten." This proselytizing technique reportedly included bullying and badgering families of Soka Gakkai members into also joining and applying undue pres-

sure on the vulnerable. Little evidence of the use of shaku-buku
has been manifest in the Nichiren Shoshu of America.

Nichiren (1222–82) taught that salvation came through the
teachings of the Lotus Sutra, a Buddhist text he believed repre-
sented Buddhism in its most primitive and pure form. Each person can attain enlightenment by being in harmony with the universal law. Happiness and peace is attained by chanting the
Daimoku, a mantra-like phrase, "namu myoho renge kyo"—that
is, "reverence for the wonderful law of the lotus"—and by recit-
ing the Lotus Sutra. Members recite the sutra and invoke repeti-
tively the Daimoku at least twice daily—morning and evening—
before the Gohonzon, an enshrined scroll on which the Daimoku
is written. Individuals may also carry a Gohonzon scroll on their
person and repeat the Daimoku as they feel led.

After coming to America in the early 1960s, the Nichiren
Shoshu experienced a rapid growth among non-Orientals in the
late sixties and spread into a national movement in the early
seventies. George N. Williams, a Caucasian, became its General
Director and led its development so that now units can be found
in most major U.S. cities.

Christian "Cults"

In the late 1960s a new revival of traditional Protestant Christianity began among the flower children who had gathered in
California. The flower culture had created a new mode of living:
"on the street." The street people walked the streets during the
day and found any convenient pad to flop on in the evening.
Their life evolved around psychedelic drugs, psychedelic art and
music, and underground newspapers.

To bring the message of salvation in Jesus to these street
people, evangelists moved onto the streets to preach and distrib-
ute their Christian underground newspapers. The early activity
of people like Duane Petersen and Don Williams sparked a national movement of young adults into conservative Christianity.
The converts became known as the Jesus People. The Jesus
People movement found quick support among mainline
churches, who at first encouraged it and later co-opted and ab-
sorbed much of it. Nevertheless, the movement produced several
new denominations.

Soon after the movement began, theological conflict developed, and some groups were denounced for their recruitment

tactics. At least four groups were accused of irregularities by the main body of Jesus People. These same groups later became the focus of anti-cult activity.

The Children of God/The Family of Love

The Children of God began as a unit of Teen Challenge, the street ministry begun by Pentecostalist David Wilkerson. David Brandt Berg led the Teen Challenge unit in Huntington Beach, California. In 1969 Berg received a revelation that California was threatened by a major earthquake, and as a result, he led his followers on an eight-month trek through the Southwest. The trek, which ended in Texas in 1970, became the constituting event for the group. They saw it as an Exodus-like journey, and Berg, now in place as an independent teacher, began to call himself Moses David.

The Children of God accept the basic framework of traditional Christianity, although deviating at several key points. They accept the writings of Moses David as an authority equal to the Bible. These writings are regularly published in a series of tracts and pamphlets called *Mo Letters*. They are communalists. Although communalism has a long and honored history in the church, after the first generations it was always a minority practice. Communal ideals have been particularly abhorrent to modern anti-cultists.

The Children of God have been most criticized for their sexual teachings. They have been accused of condoning lesbianism, using sex to attract new members, and practicing polygamy (at least in the case of Moses David). There may be some merit to the accusations, but in the heated anti-cult climate no evaluation of the scope of the practices has been possible.

The Children of God spread quickly, aided by the early movement of several prominent Jesus People into their ranks. They were also the first target of the anti-cultist's and deprogrammer Ted Patrick. In 1974 the Attorney General of the State of New York published a report of his investigation and accused them of a variety of crimes. Due partly to pressure put on them in the United States, the Children of God moved many of their members out of the United States to Europe and Latin America. Moses David himself moved first to Puerto Rico and more recently settled in London. World headquarters were moved to Switzerland. As of 1980, less than 500 members remain in the United

States. They also recently changed their name to the Family of Love.

The Christian Foundation

The Christian Foundation's work preceded the main phase of the Jesus People revival by several years and was for a while an integral part of it. They were one in doctrine with the mainline of the movement. They differed from much of the mainline by their separatism, their high pressure evangelism, and the strict communal discipline to which members adhered.

Tony and Susan Alamo began the Foundation in 1967. Both had been reared as Jews. To pursue a singing career Tony had changed his name from Bernie Lazar Hoffman. With the help of the Full Gospel Businessmen's Fellowship International, a lay Pentecostal group, the Alamos established their Foundation's headquarters on a ranch near Saugus, California, from where they launched preaching missions into Los Angeles.

People attracted by the Alamos' ministry were invited to spend a weekend at the ranch. Conflict developed when people returned from these weekends and accused the Alamos of keeping them virtual prisoners and badgering them to convert by using highly manipulative techniques.

In the midst of growing criticism the Alamos pulled up stakes and shifted their center of activity to a small town in Arkansas, where they own and operate several businesses. They also opened a Western clothing store in Nashville, Tennessee. In recent years they have toned down their evangelism efforts and kept the Foundation somewhat isolated. As they have moved into a more settled condition, the criticism and controversy have lessened considerably.

The Local Church

The Local Church (a title given to this group by outsiders) was begun in China by a lay evangelist, Watchman Nee. The movement spread in pre-Maoist China. Nee was arrested by the Communist government in 1952 and spent the last 20 years of his life in prison.

Nee's theology derived from the Plymouth Brethren, whose fundamentalist teaching permeated Protestantism in the late 19th century. The Brethren emphasized dispensationalism, a method of viewing Bible history as a series of different dispensations or periods of God's differing activity in the world. The Brethren opposed denominational Christianity. Nee's particular variation on this ecclesiastical theme gave the group its name. He believed there could be only one true church in any one community. The local church is the gathering of all Christians in a particular area.

Nee has rarely been accused of heresy—at least on any major issue—and his books can be found in Christian bookstores. Possibly the most distinctive doctrinal deviation is their practice of multiple baptisms, which they call "burying." They baptize a member as many times as he or she feels the need to bury the "old man" within. Main criticism of the group comes from other Christians who have accused the Local Church of "sheep-stealing" among their members and of disrupting gatherings of non-Local Church people.

The Local Church has congregations in most cities across North America, but they have kept a low profile. Evangelism is done primarily by word of mouth and few items of their own publications go to nonmembers. Hence, most people rarely hear of their presence. Headquarters are at the Church in Anaheim, California.

Way International

Like the Local Church, the Way International was in existence for many years before the Jesus People revival but for several years was considered an integral part of the revival. Like the Children of God, however, the Way was denounced by the mainstream of the Jesus People movement for its doctrinal distinctiveness, particularly the Way's belief that Jesus is not God, that the dead are not alive until Christ's return, and that every born-again believer can and should manifest all the gifts of the Spirit (mentioned in 1 Corinthians 12).

The Way International was founded in 1942 as the Vesper Chimes, but its name was changed in 1955 to the Way, Inc. and later to the Way International, in 1975. The Way's founder, Victor Paul Wierwille, was at that time a minister of the Evangelical and Reformed Church (now part of the United Church of Christ) but resigned from that body in 1957.

The Way International is organized on the model of a tree, from the Root (international headquarters) to Trunks (national organizations) to Limbs (state and province organizations) to

Branches (organizations in cities and towns) to Twigs (small, individual fellowship groups). Individual members are likened to Leaves. New members usually come into the Way through taking the basic 12-session course developed by Wierwille, called "Power for Abundant Living," in which the teachings of the Way are presented. Several options are open to graduates of the course. Many continue to attend Twig fellowships. Others become more involved by attending the Way College, in Emporia, Kansas; by joining the Way Corps; or by becoming a "Way over the World Ambassador" for one year. Each program is designed to give practical application to the Way's biblical teachings.

The Way considers itself to be a biblical research, teaching, and household fellowship ministry. It neither builds nor owns any church buildings but rather meets in home fellowships. Often overlooked by those who write about the Way's development is the role that Wierwille's research in Aramaic has played. He was spurred on by his contact with and personal relationship to Dr. George M. Lamsa, translator of the Lamsa Bible. Among the activities of the Way have been the establishment of a large Aramaic facility (completely computerized) and the training of a group of scholars in the Aramaic (Syrian) language.

Like the Local Church, the Way teaches a form of dispensationalism, although Wierwille prefers the term administration. According to Wierwille, we (present believers) live under the Church administration that began at Pentecost. Scripture from before Pentecost is not addressed to the Church but is for our learning. Pre-Pentecost scripture includes the Old Testament, the Four Gospels, the epistles of Hebrews and James, and Acts (which serves as a transition volume). The Gospels belong to the previous Christ Administration.

Doctrinally, the Way could be considered both Arian and Pentecostal. It rejects the Trinitarian orthodoxy of most of Western Christianity. It believes in the divinity of Jesus, the divine conception of Jesus by God, and that he is the Son of God but not God the Son. It also believes in receiving the fullness of the Holy Spirit, God's power, which may be evidenced by the nine manifestations of the Spirit: speaking in tongues, interpretation of tongues, prophecy, word of knowledge, word of wisdom, discerning of spirits, faith (believing), miracles, and healing.

Criticism of the Way has been mounting and intense. Most has focused on the standard anti-cult theme, accusing the Way of brainwashing and Wierwille of growing rich off the movement. A prime additional criticism claims that Wierwille has been training the Way members in the use of deadly weapons for possible future violent activity against the group's enemies. This criticism derived from the Way College's cooperation with the State of Kansas program to promote hunting safety, in which all students had the choice (but were not required) to enroll. No evidence of any violent motivations, intent, or actions has been produced to back up this harsh criticism.

Headquarters of the Way International are in New Knoxville, Ohio, on the site of the homestead where Dr. Wierwille was born. The Wierwille family donated the farm and lands to the Way International organization, and an expansive center has developed. An annual gathering, the Rock of Ages, is held there and attracts followers in the tens of thousands from both the United States and abroad.

The Unification Church

The Unification Church (full name: The Holy Spirit Association for the Unification of World Christianity) is the essence of what constitutes a cult in the mind of popular anti-cultism. From the Unification Church come such terms as heavenly deception and love bombing. While becoming the best-known cult in America, its leader, the Rev. Sun Myung Moon, has become one of the ten most hated men in the land. To understand the controversy that has surrounded the Church it is necessary to look first at its history and beliefs.

The Unification Church was founded in 1954, in Seoul, Korea, by Reverend Moon. Eighteen years earlier he had had a vision of Jesus, who told him that he would have a mission to perform. In subsequent years Moon discovered the Divine Principle from which the teachings of the Church derive. The Church was brought to the United States in 1959 but did not experience significant growth until the 1970s, when Moon began a series of national preaching tours and eventually moved to the United States.

The teachings found literary expression in a book, the *Divine Principle,* which has gone through several editions in an attempt to present the Principle more accurately. The teachings begin in the understanding of creation.

The Unification Church teaches that the Infinite God can be known by the study of His Creation. Everything exists in pairs—

masculine and feminine, positive and negative, initiative and receptive. God contains the same polarity. All things also contain an inner and outer nature. In like measure, God's Internal Nature (Sung-sang) is His heart of infinite love, and His External Form (Hyung-sang) is the energy of the universe.

God created the universe to bring Himself joy and to bring joy to humanity. All men and women have the capacity to reflect fully the image of God and become one with Him. Oneness is achieved when individuals develop fully their capacity to love. In family life one ideally finds the most complete expression of the range and depth of human love. God's love is the infinite counterpart of the three modes of human love: love of parents for children, love of husband and wife, and love of children for parents.

Because God is the substantial being of goodness and the eternal idea in accordance with His purpose, humans were also created to become ideal embodiments of goodness, in whom sin and suffering would be a contradiction and an impossibility. The reality of the contradictions and evil in which humans find themselves is a result of having lost the original value by falling.

Having fallen into sin, humans must tread the path of salvation under God's blessing; in the Unification Principle, salvation is restoration. In other words, the purpose of salvation is to return to the original state before the fall; therefore, God's providence of salvation is the providence of restoration. In this restoration process, Christ comes as the mediator and the example of how to live spiritually and physically to become God's ideal. Therefore, by uniting the heart and action with Christ, people are "saved."

The teachings postulate that Jesus was supposed to take a bride and create the ideal family, but his early death limited this plan. In essence Jesus fell short of completing his assigned task and the first Advent brought only "spiritual" salvation and a promise to return. The Lord of the Second Advent will bring "physical" salvation. To church members, the Second Coming is at hand and Reverend Moon is the prophet whose revelation and work are preparing the way.

A spiritual world exists as the counterpart of the physical. In the physical world we as humans mature our spirits within the limits of time so we will be prepared to live with God eternally. Heaven is the highest level of the spiritual world where perfected people dwell in oneness with God.

The Unification Church is organized hierarchically. It is

headed by Reverend Moon and an international board of directors. A national president is named for each country and is directly accountable to the board and Reverend Moon. In the United
States, state and local leaders are appointed by the president. The
national Church also controls the various departments of Church
activity. For example, the Church operates a medical mission program in West Africa, which is conducted from the national headquarters in New York City.

THE STRANGERS AMONG US[2]

Every so often the veil lifts and, for an instant, the dark matter
in the spiritual universe becomes visible. Jim Jones and more than
900 followers die by their own hands at Jonestown, Guyana.
Charles Manson's murderous "family" slaughters pregnant ac-
tress Sharon Tate and six others in Southern California. Then
this February, a bloody shoot-out at the Waco compound of David
Koresh and his Branch Davidians claims the lives of four federal
agents. It is comforting to imagine that such tragedies always
happen somewhere else, and that the groups responsible couldn't
possibly be living next door. But sometimes they are.

According to J. Gordon Melton, author of *Encyclopedic Handbook of Cults in America*, there are at least 700 cults active in the
U.S., a number that has been rising steadily since the turn of the
century. Though it is difficult to say what constitutes a cult, such
groups have several features in common. Chief among them is
the members' dependence on a single, messianic leader who frequently makes all the decisions that govern their lives. Rational
thought is discouraged, often by mind-numbing rituals and sensory deprivation. Recruits are smothered with "love," then manipulated through guilt.

From the outside, the lure of these fringe groups can be difficult
to understand. Indeed, many former cult members can't explain it
either. Generally, says Ronald Enroth, a sociology professor at
Westmont College in Santa Barbara, Calif., and author of the book
Churches That Abuse, cult leaders "reach out to the disaffected in our

[2]Article by Elizabeth Gleick, et al. From *People Weekly* 39:34–9 Ap 19 '93. Copyright © 1993 by Time, Inc. Reprinted with permission.

society, people who have been marginalized, who don't fit in. [The leader] tells them, 'We're God's special people.'" What follows is a look at five such groups—and how they work.

A Renegade Swami in Custody

Keith Ham is the kind of guru who gives cults a bad name. Back in 1987 the international Hare Krishna governing body expelled Ham—who prefers to be called His Divine Grace Kirtanananda Swami Bhaktipada—on the grounds that he was a "greedy megalomaniac." The verdict of the federal courts is even harsher: In 1991 Ham was sentenced to 30 years in prison for authorizing beating, kidnapping and murder to cover up his personal sect's illegal multimillion-dollar activities, which included counterfeiting and selling trademarked products such as Snoopy T-shirts, bumper stickers and caps.

But neither the convictions, which Bhaktipada is appealing, nor allegations of neglect and sexual abuse of children in the sect have discredited him in the eyes of more than 300 faithful at New Vrindaban, the 4,000-acre commune near Moundsville, W.Va., which he founded 24 years ago. "There's a feeling that it's legalized religious persecution," said commune spokesman Gadadhar Das. Devotees of the 55-year-old swami, a Baptist minister's son from Peekskill, N.Y., continue to seek fusion with God through chanting Krishna's name hundreds of times a day, refraining from eating meat, from gambling and from sex—except for procreation within Bhaktipada-sanctioned marriage. Meanwhile the schismatic Krishnas run one of the state's largest tourist attractions. Each year more than 60,000 of the curious pay $5 to see Prabhupada's Palace of Gold, a glittering gold-domed monument to the founder of the Hare Krishna sect, and its gardens featuring 1,000 varieties of roses.

A victim of childhood polio, Bhaktipada walks with canes and is confined to an apartment in Wheeling, some 12 miles from the commune. It is not his disability that keeps him there, but a federal court order—plus the electronic ankle bracelet he must wear pending the outcome of his appeal.

The Guru Who Calls Herself Ma

In 1977 Deborah and John (these are pseudonyms) traveled at the suggestion of their marital therapists to a 47-acre ranch in Roseland, Fla., near Palm Beach, run by an obscure religious group. Soon after their arrival, the couple found themselves in the thrall of Ma Jaya Bhagavati Cho (known simply as Ma) and her Kashi Church. Ma, explains Deborah, is "brilliant. She can know your innermost secrets, and people see this gift and think she must be divine."

In reality, Ma is Joyce Green Difiore Cho, a 52-year-old former Jewish housewife from Brooklyn who says that in 1973, while meditating as part of a weight-loss program, she had visitations from Christ, whose word she began spreading, and later, visions of Hindu leader Neem Karoli Baba, who is still her guru today. Daily life on her ashram, says Ma's spokesman, John Evans, emphasizes service to the community, and Ma does, in fact, spend a great deal of time visiting local nursing homes and AIDS patients. Deborah, however, insists that many ashram activities are aimed at "stopping your mind" and consuming all free time. Among them, she says, are early morning meditations, all-night meetings and long hours of work on or off the ranch. Members are not allowed to have sexual relations except for purposes of procreation.

According to Deborah, Ma also allegedly persuaded her and others to give their children to Ma to raise. In 1981, when John and Deborah had a baby, Deborah says Ma induced her to forge Ma's name on the birth certificate—a charge Ma has denied. Then, says Deborah, she was permitted only limited contact with her daughter. John and Deborah left the ashram in 1982 and returned home to Colorado, leaving their daughter behind. "My daughter was to succeed Joyce," explains Deborah. "I believed it, as ridiculous as it sounds." With the help of a court order and a SWAT team, they retrieved the child in 1989; she is now in sixth grade in Colorado.

Ma has a few hundred followers, some 150 of whom live at the ashram. Folksinger Arlo Guthrie, who keeps a room there, has been a member for seven years. Two of his four children attend the ashram school. Says Guthrie: "I love Ma. She has never asked me for money for herself—only to help other people. She serves God by serving man." Deborah, of course, disagrees. And she worries about the children who have grown up on the ashram. "They haven't seen much of the outside world," she says. "They think she's God. That horrifies me."

A Cult for the Computer Age

He promises six-figure salaries, fancy cars and enlightenment through his peculiar blend of Buddhism and capitalism. But life inside the decade-old group nicknamed the Computer Cult, run by Frederick Lenz III, 43, also known as Zen Master Rama, is very different, former followers say.

Almost all the money his 300-plus disciples on the East Coast and in California earn from their jobs in the computer field—an estimated $4 million to $10 million a year—is reportedly funneled back to the so-called Yuppie Guru through required monthly meditation and computer-programming seminars. While the San Diego-born guru enjoys a sumptuous lifestyle at mansions in Santa Fe, Malibu and on Long Island, Lenzites live in Spartan apartments wherever they work. Instead of enlightenment, say disaffected former members, there is constant fear.

"He teaches that the rest of society is evil," says Mark Lurtsema, 32, a New York City computer programmer who followed Lenz for six years. According to Lurtsema, Lenz convinces followers that only his occult powers can shield them from demons and other dark forces. Lurtsema says the blond six-footer rules over every aspect of his followers' lives, from clothing (red and black are power colors) to cars (owned or leased Mercedes—but not the 500 model, which only Lenz is allowed to drive). Female erstwhile cult members claim Lenz pressures them into sex. (Lenz declines to be interviewed. But his press kit accuses those making "false and defamatory statements" about the group of "bias, unreliability and bad faith.")

"I realized I was looking for an easy answer," confesses Lurtsema, who left the group three years ago with his wife-to-be. "He formats people like floppy disks. I didn't have my own game plan, so I played his game."

An Elusive Pastor Reborn

In 1982, when Betsy Dovydenas was 30, she was searching for a new spiritual path. Heir to the Dayton-Hudson department store fortune, Dovydenas joined the Bible Speaks, a Lenox, Mass., group headed by Carl H. Stevens Jr., a one-time bakery-truck driver. "I was sleep-deprived, food-deprived," says Dovydenas. "They worked on me night and day." The mesmerizing Stevens urged Dovydenas to leave her husband and two children, she says, and to donate $6.6 million to his group over three years. But in 1986 Dovydenas's husband, Jonas, her parents, and a "cult deprogrammer" managed to pry her away from the group. In 1987 she sued the church for her money—and though she won, it was a moral victory alone, as the Bible Speaks had already declared bankruptcy. Soon afterward a police raid on the Lenox headquarters turned up $60,000 worth of weapons and electronic surveillance equipment.

Meanwhile the sect was reincarnated—Carl Stevens now preaches his version of Christianity to some 1,400 faithful at the Greater Grace World Outreach headquarters in Baltimore. Michael Marr, Stevens' attorney, points out that Stevens does not even collect a salary (though some followers do pay him fees for business consulting). "He's a genius when it comes to understanding the word of God," says Marr. "To call him a cult leader is a lie from the pit of hell."

Michael Gray, 33, a Bel Air, Md., automotive sales consultant, takes a darker view of Stevens. He stopped attending Greater Grace services after six months, concerned by "the constant messages that Stevens was being persecuted because he was 'God's man.'" The pastor often arrived at church flanked by armed bodyguards. Gray feared "what could happen when levels of paranoia reach such a heightened state." He didn't wait to find out.

The Piecemakers: Blessed—Or Abused?

The Piecemakers Country Store in Costa Mesa, Calif., offers everything a crafts lover could ask for: quilts, sewing classes, an old-fashioned candy counter—and a chance to walk with Jesus. "It was really neat in the beginning," says Marion Simonds, 62, about Piecemakers, a booming retail business cum Christian sect that began 20 years ago as a Bible-study group in the home of Marie Kolasinski. "We all came and fellowshipped together." But soon, say estranged members, Kolasinski, 72, began preaching communal living, no sex and limited communication among family members in order to bring her followers closer to God. "Marie used to say, 'If you're not miserable, if your flesh isn't being put to death, then God isn't dealing with you,'" recalls Paula Foster, 44, who after 11 years broke away from Piecemakers in 1982. Kolasinski, for her part, is said to deal with her flock by cursing at and humiliating members in front of the group. "She believes God is very intense," explains Foster. "He's a God that kicks you in the ass all the time." Kolasinski's hold over her members is such that Simonds and her husband, Harold, 63, signed over the title to their home to Piecemakers in 1986 and only won it back in

1992 after a yearlong legal battle. "We're totally harmless," insists Kolasinski, who says that the Simondses gave up their house freely. "We're people that love the Lord. You don't find that too much in this country."

THE GREAT AMERICAN CULT CONTROVERSY[3]

No one who saw the grisly photographs soon will forget the sight of hundreds of swollen corpses, strewn about like piles of refuse in the fields of an isolated South American settlement. The dead were followers of the Reverend Jim Jones, an intense, charismatic figure whose one-time vision of a just society had degenerated into paranoia and madness. Jones' flock, bound to their leader psychologically, economically, and geographically, obediently had joined him in a last bizarre act of communion, ladling out cyanide-laced servings of Flavour-Aid to one another.

It has been more than 13 years since the Guyana massacre that left more than 900 cult members, three investigative reporters, and a U.S. Congressman dead. The public uproar over "mind-controlling cults" has died down, but the complex moral and legal dilemmas raised in the aftermath of Jonestown have not gone away. They remain at the heart of two cherished—and potentially conflicting —American values: the right to seek one's own version of religious truth in whatever manner one chooses, however unconventional; and the right to be free from coercion and manipulation in the name of someone else's version of religious truth.

Ironically, the Jonestown tragedy concluded a decade in which the highly visible presence and rapid growth of alternative or unconventional religious groups had engendered excitement among many observers of American religion. There are several reasons for the sudden high profile of unconventional groups. One was President Lyndon Johnson's repeal of the so-called Oriental Exclusion Acts, which brought a wave of new immigrants—

[3]Article by Elizabeth C. Nordbeck, dean of faculty, Andover Newton Theological School. From *U.S.A. Today magazine* 78–80 S '92. Copyright © 1992 by U.S.A. Today. Reprinted with permission.

and their unfamiliar religious traditions—from the East. A second was the ongoing effect of the youthful counterculture movement of the 1960s. Still another was the phenomenon of rapid cultural change and dislocation, and the accompanying search for what sociologist Robert Bellah has called "a meaningful pattern of personal and social existence." So widespread was the perception of radical change in the landscape of traditional faith that some hopeful observers hailed the dawn of a "new religious consciousness" that could revitalize America's languishing religious institutions.

However, these hopes were not shared by everyone. Early in the 1970s, pockets of resistance to groups like David "Moses" Berg's controversial Children of God, Sun Myung Moon's Unification Church, and Jim Jones' People's Temple already had risen. At first, membership consisted mainly of the parents and friends of persons recruited into these unconventional religious movements. Throughout the decade, however, many local anti-cult organizations became aware of one another, primarily through reports in the mass media. Members discovered that they shared a variety of concerns and experiences. Soon, an informal coalition for support, communication, and resourcing emerged.

Today, the so-called Anti-Cult Movement comprises a loose national and international network of organizations with names like the American Family Foundation, the Cult Awareness Network, and the International Cult Education Program. In addition to the families of cult "victims," its expanded membership includes law enforcement personnel, clergy, social scientists, medical professionals, and evangelical Christians, as well as apostates (ex-cultists, many of whom have been "deprogrammed" or counseled out of their respective religious groups).

Conflicting Claims

The claims of the Anti-Cult Movement are simple: Mind-controlling cults are on the rise, representing a real danger to young people, families, and—increasingly—the elderly. Cult leaders are exploitive, manipulative, and self-aggrandizing; some, like Jim Jones, are sick. Their members often have been socially conditioned, or brainwashed, into unquestioning acquiescence and obedience. A body of "apostate literature," written by ex-cultists, seems to corroborate allegations of forcible detainment, sensory deprivation, and other coercive techniques de-

signed to enforce conformity. The solution, maintain anti-cult
spokesmen, is to educate the public about the danger of cults,
"free" individual members whenever possible, and restrain these
groups' activities by all available legal means.

Countering the claims of anti-cult activists is the testimony of
a growing body of independent scholars, mental health professionals, clergy, and civil libertarians who argue that, in fact, there
is no widespread cult threat. Not all cults are dangerous, nor are
cult leaders invariably charlatans or psychopaths. Even more important, there is no convincing evidence that a manipulative process called brainwashing actually exists, let alone offers religious
groups an effective tool for entrapment. Attempts to deprogram
or counsel persons out of their religious affiliations, it is maintained, can do more long-term psychological damage than simply
leaving them alone. Moreover, attempts to limit the pursuit of
religious freedom to conventional religious practices are uncon-
stitutional.

Who is right here? The answer is not immediately evident,
and emotions run high on both sides. As one exploratory study,
sponsored by the Jewish Community Relations Council of Philadelphia during the 1980s, observed, "We found that it was a relatively simple matter to find outspoken individuals with strong
feelings about cults. But, invariably, if these people knew anything about cults it was because they were advocates and not
observers—cult members, deprogrammed former cult members,
the deprogrammers themselves, parents whose children were in
cults. These people's stories were important, but they were far
from objective." Research scholars, on the other hand, have been
accused of being *too* objective. Concerned with patterns of behavior, with raw data and not with value judgments, theological
truths, or pastoral concerns, their approaches admittedly have
failed to deal with what many believe is the high human cost of
cult involvement: shattered families, broken marriages, and disillusioned individuals.

If public attitude is any measure, anti-cultists so far have had
the upper hand in this debate. Popular anti-cult literature is on
the shelves of churches and libraries across the country. Cults are
feared widely and generally assumed to be growing and dangerous.

Meanwhile, critics of anti-cult claims have a point. The emergence of cults is no sudden, late-20th-century phenomenon. Historically, new and unfamiliar religious movements (including

Christianity itself) have emerged periodically and always have generated fear and antagonism disproportionate to their real threat. In 19th-century America, new sects such as the Mormons, Christian Scientists, Jehovah's Witnesses, and Shakers engendered widespread opposition and, occasionally, violence. Even the Roman Catholic Church—no cult, but popularly linked in the early 1800s with fear of "the power of Rome" and mistrust of foreigners—endured harassment and mob attacks.

With time and familiarity, suspicion of these groups has abated, and they have adapted more or less comfortably to their surrounding culture. A familiar example of this sort of mutual accommodation is the Shakers. The remaining handful of quiet, elderly members in Maine and New Hampshire are regarded sympathetically, even nostalgically, by the general public. In their heyday, however, the Shakers were as unconventional as any of today's new cults. Living in celibate communities under the charismatic leadership of a female Messiah figure, they pursued a spartan, agrarian lifestyle, relieved only by the energetic rituals of dance and song from which they acquired their name.

Critics also point out that accusations of a sinister and sophisticated process called brainwashing are questionable at best. The term dates from the Korean War, when Chinese communists claimed to have brainwashed American prisoners-of-war through a coercive process of "thought reform," or attitude change. Evidently, the communists were not very successful reformers. In *The Mind Manipulators*, Alan Scheflen and Edward Opton note that only about one percent of the 3,500 Americans held captive ever made any statements supporting communism. By comparison, two percent of Union soldiers captured during the Civil War—long before the advent of brainwashing—joined the Confederate Army. If, as anti-cultists claim, cult leaders rely heavily on brainwashing for recruitment and group maintenance, their "victims" have little to fear.

Social scientific studies of cult defectors also tend to confirm the fluidity of movement in and out of these groups. Some 90% of cult joiners voluntarily leave within two or three years of entering, a finding that challenges the familiar depiction of cults as fortress-like enclaves of repression from which victims can exit only through outside intervention.

Still, serious questions remain. If it is *not* really possible to wipe the mind clean of its former attachments and ideas and replace them with new ones, how can we account for the apparent alterations in the behavior of persons who join unconventional religious groups? What makes a middle-class college student shave his head, don saffron robes, and retire to a communal farm where he will rise each morning at three a.m. to chant before going to the fields?

There always have been a variety of reasons why men and women are attracted to unconventional religions: dissatisfaction with their present lives, idealism, a need for personal boundaries, the quest for concrete answers to spiritual questions, even the acquisition of a stable network of friendships. Some few who enter these groups are emotionally needy or frankly disturbed (and, typically, the cult is held accountable for their sickness when they exit). For many, the attraction is the discipline and distinctiveness of the group itself.

Certainly all cults—contrary to portrayals in the popular media—are not alike. Nevertheless, by definition, they exist "over against," or in tension with, whatever is typical or normative in their surrounding culture. Like others that do not reflect common patterns of behavior, for their survival, cults must seek to replace members' old habits and ideas with new, group-reinforcing ones.

This is accomplished through a familiar (and not at all mysterious) process of socialization, which may include exposure to new language, dress, daily habits, and ritual practices, as well as strong peer pressure to conform. This process can be described, quite accurately, as indoctrination, and it is offensive to Americans for whom autonomy, individualism, and self-determination are basic values. Yet, if cults are to be criticized for indoctrinating, we also must criticize numerous evangelical Christian denominations, commercial enterprises such as Amway, Roman Catholic religious orders, and the U.S. military, all of which routinely use the same kinds of processes and pressures to reinforce group standards.

Opponents of the Anti-Cult Movement are particularly critical of the interventionist tactics some activists insist are necessary to free cult "victims" from their emotional and psychological dependencies. Today, the tactics of physical restraint used by pioneer deprogrammer Ted Patrick have been modified—due, in part, to the lawsuits brought by unsuccessfully deprogrammed cult members. More common are "exit therapies" which seek, through intensive (but presumably voluntary) encounters, to persuade cult members of their errors.

It is true that deprogramming or exit counseling *can* move a cult member out of his or her group to the joy of family and friends, but the long-term results of intervention may be less happy. In *Leaving Cults: The Dynamics of Defection*, sociologist Stuart Wright reports that persons who are "coercively dissuaded" from their beliefs have greater difficulty re-integrating themselves into society than do those who leave voluntarily. They may be "turned off" religion permanently. They also are much more likely to have negative, rather than neutral or mixed, feelings about their own cult experiences—a finding that helps explain the number of deprogrammed persons who become anti-cult activists or deprogrammers themselves.

Religious Liberty

Perhaps the most trenchant criticism of anti-cult activities concerns the issue of religious liberty. The First Amendment ("Congress shall make no law respecting an establishment of religion, or prohibiting the free exercise thereof") guarantees Americans the right to worship as they please. Anti-cultists correctly point out that their negative assessment of cultic groups does not indicate a rejection of religious freedom. Historically, however, it often has been a dangerously short step from negative assessments to restriction and repression.

The problem is that the freedoms guaranteed by the Constitution never have been absolute. In actual practice, the "religion clause" has meant that, although people may *believe* whatever they want, they are permitted to *manifest* their beliefs only insofar as their behavior is not deemed harmful to others or the common moral foundations that are the basis of American society. In some cases, this limitation is fairly clear, if controversial. Adult Christian Scientists and Jehovah's Witnesses legally may refuse medical help or blood transfusions for themselves, but they may not be able to do the same for their underage children. In other cases, however, determining whether something is harmful, and to whom, may be much more difficult. An example:

In the mid 1980s, Rep. Robert Walker (R.-Pa.) proposed legislation that would have denied tax-exempt status to practitioners of witchcraft, which he defined as having to do with "the use of evil spirits, the supernatural and sorcery with malicious intent." Friends and members of "The Craft" objected. Their religion, they pointed out, recently had enjoyed a revival, primarily among feminists disaffected from male-centered traditional faiths. To deny it tax-exempt status would effectually be sex discrimination. It would single out one set of beliefs as not worthy of the protected status enjoyed by other, more popular beliefs. Most critical to practitioners was the question of who, ultimately, has the right to define the real nature of witchcraft—or, for that matter, of any religious group.

Contemporary witches describe their faith as having to do not with evil spirits or malicious activity as Walker suggested but with the cycles of nature, the relationship of human beings and the natural world, and with healing through the use of both natural and supernatural means. Whose definition is correct, Walker's or the witches'? Whose should be heard? The witches (or any conventional or unconventional religious groups) do *not* have a fundamental right to define who they are and what they believe, essential principles of religious freedom have been abrogated. It is the tendency of anti-cultists to position themselves, with Walker, as arbiters of legality and legitimacy, to claim knowledge of the "real" nature and purpose of unconventional groups, that most angers their detractors.

Still, even the most stringent critic eventually must come to terms with Jonestown as not the only example of new religion run amok. There also are Bhagwan Shree Rajneesh with his Rolls Royces, Charles Manson's "family," Philadelphia's MOVE, among others. Violence, brutality, extortion, misrepresentation, spouse and child abuse—these undeniably are part of the story of contemporary cults. They are, of course, part of the story of traditional religions, too. In the latter groups, however, common standards and structures of discipline and order tend to limit, if not entirely eliminate, the potential for criminal activity and abuse.

In the end, it may be that the public must learn from both defenders and critics of cults. Nineteen ninety-two marks the 300th anniversary of the Salem witchcraft trials, that infamous episode in which a desire for orthodoxy and order triumphed over common sense and resulted in the deaths of 19 people. Today, we dare not be too hasty in asking lawyers and legislators to restrict the activities of religious groups that are antagonistic to normative American values, let alone merely different. Our own history of repression and brutality in the name of religious "truth" and cultural homogeneity is too recent and too painful.

Neither should Americans be victims of their own freedom. Perhaps, as anti-cultists suggest, the answer is to educate the public about the dangers of cults. If so, our presentations must be historically, sociologically, and psychologically sound, representing the research and conclusions of both anti-cultists and cult defenders. They must include the testimony of well-adjusted cult members as well as angry apostates. This means they can not be founded on assumptions that are fundamentally ideological or partisan. Nor can would-be teachers use the truth-claims and traditions of their own faiths as a tacit measure of other groups' legitimacy.

Ultimately, the cult threat—if there is one—probably is met best by informed individuals, secure in their knowledge *and* their right to choose, as others have before them, unconventional ways of worship.

WACO REVISITED[4]

The Justice and Treasury Departments are now releasing their reports on the circumstances leading up to the incineration of eighty-six Branch Davidians outside Waco on April 19. The Treasury's Bureau of Alcohol, Tobacco and Firearms, which is taking the main fall, deserves everything it gets, but should be joined in the scapegoats' gallery by the F.B.I. and by Attorney General Janet Reno.

One of the outside experts recruited by the Justice and Treasury Departments to review the case and peruse internal documents was Professor Nancy Ammerman of the Candler School of Theology at Emory University. Ammerman gives short shrift to the A.T.F., which made no effort to solicit dispassionate insight into the nature of the Davidians before raiding their compound in February and thus instigating the grim drama. The F.B.I. was similarly brusque, resolving by mid-March to have no more truck with "Bible babble": make no effort, that is, to comprehend Koresh's frame of reference. The F.B.I. did consult one person in religious studies, Glenn Hilburn, chairman of the religion department at Baylor. He offered sound counsel but was ignored.

But from the F.B.I.'s own Behavioral Science Services Unit,

[4]Article by Alexander Cockburn. From *The Nation* 257:414–15 O 18 '93. Copyright © 1993 by The Nation. Reprinted with permission of the author.

Pete Smerick along with Special Agent Mark Young cautioned their superiors that a "show of force will draw David Koresh and his followers closer together in the 'bunker mentality' and they would rather die than surrender." They too were ignored, in favor of the bureau's special agents in charge—people, Ammerman says, who considered religious beliefs "usually a convenient cover for criminal activity."

Ammerman also confirms, after scrutinizing A.T.F. and F.B.I. records, that career "cult hunters" were deeply involved in the government's assaults. She says a man named Rick Ross "clearly had the most extensive access to both agencies of any person on the 'cult expert' list and he was apparently listened to more attentively." The F.B.I. interview report noted that Ross has a personal hatred for all religious cults and would willingly aid law enforcement in an attempt to "destroy a cult." The A.T.F., Ammerman discloses, "interviewed the persons [Ross] directed them to and evidently used information from those interviews in planning their February 28 raid."

Now, Ross is a man who boasts of having performed many "deprogrammings" down the years. He was frequently interviewed by the media as an "expert" during the siege, and indeed figured prominently in the *Waco Tribune-Herald* series on the Branch Davidians that started February 27. On February 26 the paper informed the A.T.F. that the series would begin the next day, a Saturday. The A.T.F. duly launched its raid on Sunday, in the shadow of the *Tribune-Herald*'s series headline, "The Sinful Messiah."

Ross acquired at least some of his assertions about the group from deprogramming sessions in mid-1992 with a former member of the Branch Davidians, David Block, conducted in the Los Angeles home of Priscilla Coates, head of the Southern California chapter of the Cult Awareness Network. Evidently Ross or someone else at the sessions transmitted Block's assertions about the Waco compound to federal law enforcement. Block's name as a source is all over the initial search warrant presented by the A.T.F. to a Waco judge.

So the sponsors of the first bloody, entirely unnecessary assault on the Branch Davidians included people—the Cult Awareness Network and Ross—who, as Ammerman remarks in her report to the Justice and Treasury Departments, "have a direct ideological (and financial) interest in arousing suspicion and antagonism against what they call 'cults'." To such sponsors we should add the name of the *Waco Tribune-Herald*.

Ross is currently facing charges of unlawful imprisonment in the state of Washington, arising out of his forcible detention of another intended deprogramming victim. Ross has a history of emotional disturbance and is also a convicted jewel thief, a fact known—so Ammerman tells me—to the feds when they used him as their prime consultant. Ross's record probably inspired confidence, since police and criminals in many ways share the same psychic turf.

The relationship between the Cult Awareness Network and such deprogrammers as Ross is inevitably murky, the network being aware that felonies are sometimes part of the deprogramming menu. Another deprogrammer, Galen Kelly, who worked in security for the network for a while, has just drawn seven years and three months without parole for kidnapping a woman in Maryland who, he had the mortification to discover, was merely the roommate of his intended target.

But Cynthia Kisser, executive director of the network's national office, has called Ross "among the half dozen best deprogrammers in the country." Priscilla Coates was quoted alongside Ross in the February 27 *Waco-Tribune-Herald* as saying the Branch Davidians were "unsafe or destructive." In April, Patricia Ryan, president of the Cult Awareness Network, was quoted in the *Houston Chronicle* as saying Koresh should be arrested, using lethal force if necessary.

Ammerman makes some sensible recommendations about treatment of religious groups, which could usefully be studied by the press as well as the Justice and Treasury Departments:

[The government agents] should have understood the pervasiveness of religious experimentation in American history and the fundamental right of groups like the Davidians to practice their religion. . . . They should have understood that many new religious movements do indeed ask for commitments that seem abnormal to most of us, and these commitments do mean the disruption of "normal" family and work lives. . . . They should also understand that the vast majority of those who make such commitments do so voluntarily. The notion of "cult brainwashing" has been thoroughly discredited in the academic community. . . .

And what of Attorney General Janet Reno?

Did one have to be an academic "expert," like Professor Ammerman, to understand what a religious group might do under pressure? Does one have to be a military "expert" to understand that the firing of CS gas into a house full of children is a bad idea? The ultimate irony is that Reno emerged from the Waco holocaust with enhanced reputation, as if "taking responsibility" is such a rare moral commodity in American political life that it has to be rewarded, however deficient the action for which that responsibility is assumed.

One chilling bottom line is that the deprogramming strategies of the Cult Awareness Network are highly reminiscent of the strategies used by Reno on supposed child-abusers, breaking Ileana Fuster and trying to break Bobby Fijnje, coercing them toward mental disintegration.

THE SOCIAL ADAPTATION OF MARGINAL RELIGIOUS MOVEMENTS IN AMERICA[5]

The "cult controversy" has mellowed, but scholarly interest in marginal religious movements (MRMs) continues, with its focus shifting from earlier descriptive studies of MRMs and the social controversy surrounding them to more conceptual and theoretical issues. This article continues these developments by explicating one dimension of movement-environment relations in a broader yet more coherent way than have previous studies. We examine *processes of social adaptation* of MRMs in America in both the nineteenth and twentieth centuries. We attempt a "joint venture" which is, we hope, responsive to recent calls for closer connection between religious history and the sociology of religion, and for more integration between the study of religious movements and social movements in general.

Three observations inform the focus of our analysis. *First* is America's extreme fecundity in producing MRMs, as well as their *pervasiveness* throughout United States history. Ahlstrom identified over 120 such movements in the antebellum nineteenth century, while Melton argues that there are between 500–600 MRMs today. These estimates are surely conservative. Thus, rather than being "new," the effervescence of the so-called new religions of the 1970s should be viewed as "the continuation of a venerable tradition," and as indicative of a normal rather than an excep-

[5]Article by Charles Harper and Bryan F. LeBeau. From *Sociology of Religion* 54:2 171–92. Copyright © 1993 by the Association for Sociology of Religion. Reprinted with permission of the authors.

tional state of the American system. We prefer to use the term "marginal" rather than the more conventional "new" in order to emphasize the historicity of the phenomenon.

We are aware that the term MRM is not without its problems or ambiguities. "Marginality," as we understand it, has several dimensions. A *marginal* religious group or movement is one that is small and has deviant doctrines in relationship to established religions. An MRM is peripheral to the "established" core of religious institutions in terms of power and respectability. We argue that marginality has at least four dimensions: (1) numerical, (2) ideological (or doctrinal), (3) legitimacy ("respectability") and (4) political (power). Of these dimensions we will argue that the first is most ambiguous, the second is most invariant, and that the last two are the most significant in understanding the conflicts surrounding MRMs. Our usage of marginal (vs. established) religions is similar to Bellah and Greenspahn's distinction between "established" and "emerging" groups, and Ellwood's application of the anthropological conception of "Great" and "Little" traditions to the contemporary situation.

A *second* observation is that the existence of MRMs in America has often been surrounded by intense, rancorous, and highly politicized controversy and conflict. It is not news that during the 1970s a small number of emerging MRMs (e.g., the Unification Church, Hare Krishna, Scientology, The Way, the Divine Light Movement, and the Children of God) became intensely controversial. In the "cult controversy" of the 1970s these MRMs became widely viewed as not only deviant in the sense of being peculiar, but as dangerous and malevolent, and as threatening the well-being of individuals and the social order. Similar controversies surrounded the development of the Shakers, the Mormons, and Roman Catholicism in the nineteenth century.

A *third* observation, equally true but less often noted, is that many MRMs have been able to exist and thrive while attracting little public attention, conflict, or controversy.

There has been a vast outpouring of scholarly literature about MRMs and the "cult controversy." There have been studies of *why* they develop, *where* they develop, *how* they operate internally and successfully in their environment, and the subsequent societal *reactions* that such movement provoke. There are analyses of religious movements and tensions surrounding them that continue fruitfully to use theories specific to religion itself, particularly the church-sect-cult topologies. We do not do so, not only because of the bewildering multidimensionality of these concepts, and their specific connection with the history of Christianity, but more important, because we want to use concepts that enable us to connect the analysis of religious movements with more generic analyses of social movements.

Much of the literature about religious movements "has been less concerned with the relations between religious movements and the broader social environment than with the strategies used by religious movements themselves to mobilize resources." Studies that do examine movement-environment relationships have paid far more attention to how such MRMs become controversial than to how they adapt and exist rather uncontentiously in the larger social environment. But some studies have addressed movement accommodation.

Shupe's analysis of movement accommodation (or, "how conflict matures") is framed by the resource mobilization perspective now popular among social movement scholars. This perspective assumes that movements are best understood as systems that must "mobilize" or obtain basic resources from society, such as recruits, money and property, as well as abstract resources such as public reputation and legitimacy. Shupe argues that movement-society conflict is produced when the movement's innovative or deviant resource mobilization processes threaten or violate key values in institutional arenas, and that analysts ought to expect accommodative behaviors in precisely those values and institutions. Our analysis of these issues has some similarities and differences from that of Shupe.

Instead of resource mobilization theory, our analysis begins with the central insight of Lemert's interactionist societal reaction theory of deviance, which suggests that deviance, particularly ongoing ("career" or "secondary" deviance) is caused and progressively defined by societal reaction itself. But one of the weaknesses of such interactionist and societal reaction approaches is that they fail to specify why certain characteristics or behaviors elicit either negative or positive reactions from social control agents in the first place. So like Shupe's analysis—and conventional social control perspectives—our analysis also seeks to identify key factors that may be threatened by the characteristics and behavior of MRMs. Given this, we agree with Lemert that to account for changes in the social adaptation of movements over time requires "full" interactional analysis focusing on *all* the interactants and "how individual and aggregate responses of deviants (or in our case, MRMs) through resistance, deflection, mitigation and negotiation become influences that shape the societal reaction."

We begin focusing on the outcomes of societal reaction—on *social adaptation,* a broad summary concept indicating the quality of a movement's relations with its social environment. Movement social adaptation is defined by a position on a continuum between a positive end point (*accommodation*) and a negative one (*problematization*). High accommodation means that an MRM is able to survive in a manner that avoids public controversy and hostility, while high problematization means that an MRM becomes controversial, elicits social hostility, and becomes a recognized "social problem." The clearest empirical indicator of either of these social adaptation states we will take to be the presence (or absence) of sustained conflict between the religious movement and external community agents. These two polar dimensions of social adaptation vary both among movements and across time for the same movement. While social adaptation can be understood as a structural relationship between a movement and its social environment at a given time, across time *social adaptation is an emergent and dynamic social interaction process.*

Before leaving conceptual matters, we enter two clarifications about the dimensions of social adaptation and related notions. Accommodation does not mean that a movement becomes so indistinguishable from its social environment that it disappears as an entity (assimilation), but only that it is able to survive without generating much controversy. Survival is not the same as growth, dominance, success, or social influence. We will argue, in fact, that there is no direct determinant relationship between high problematization or accommodation and viability, growth, success, and social influence. Similarly, deviance is related to but not the same as problematization. Some deviant groups and persons are problematized, others are not. Problematization is mainly a matter of becoming the object of hostility and conflict. A group or person may be viewed as quite deviant (strange, bizarre, different) and yet, as the proverbial village eccentric, may be an accepted and uncontentious part of the social landscape. Perhaps the contemporary Amish provide the best example of an MRM that is undoubtedly "deviant," but not problematized. Most of the MRMs we consider are doctrinally deviant; only some become problematized. Hampshire and Beckford (1983) have drawn a similar distinction between movements that are simply cognitively and doctrinally eccentric and those that are viewed as fundamentally threatening to the social order.

The inclusion of the term "societal" in Lemert's perspective implies that it is not limited in application, as are most interactionist and labeling perspectives, to the analysis of individual deviance and control in small-scale or microsocial contexts. We extend the scope of societal reaction theory as a broad perspective useful for understanding the dynamics of movement-society relationships. We will add few new empirical insights that are not known either by scholars of MRMs of the 1970s (the "new religions") or by students of nineteenth-century religious movements. Rather, our goals are to: (1) provide a framework for ordering similar but disparate observations about a broad range of historical and contemporary cases, (2) produce a more adequate theoretical account of factors and processes that shape social adaptation outcomes of American MRMs, and (3) do so in a way that continues to bring the study of religious movements closer to the study of social movements in general.

Social Adaptation Patterns of American MRMs

In previous research we examined in some depth the histories of three nineteenth-century MRMs (the Shakers, Mormons, and Roman Catholics) and four contemporary ones (Scientology, the Unification Church, the Hare Krishna movement, and Nichiren Shoshu Buddhism). In addition, we less systematically examined literature about other modern MRMs: EKANKAR, *est*, and Baha'i. Because of space limitations, the findings of this investigation are presented here only in summary form, though we have used selected evidence in the following theoretical argument.

Our investigation has convinced us that there are two broad but variable patterns of "social adaptation histories" among diverse American MRMs. While not necessarily most common, the pattern most commonly reported in sociological and historical literature about American MRMs is for a recently established MRM to undergo a period of intense problematization in which it is the object of popular scorn, variously taking the form of angry mobs, a hostile press, the emergence of countergroups, a hostile anti-MRM literature, and perhaps hostile reactions from officials seeking to suppress or neutralize the influence of the MRM. Following intense problematization there is typically a period in which the MRM "learns" to be more adroit about neutralizing, deflecting, and insulating itself from hostile social reaction, and during which it may become proactive in shaping a more benign public definition of itself.

This pattern of stormy, conflict-ridden beginnings and subsequent accommodation so clearly describes Shaker, Mormon, and Roman Catholic experience in America that it would be difficult to write about their adaptation histories in any different way. Indeed, Foster argues that this has been *the* pattern of religious accommodation across time in America:

Each new group has initially aroused suspicion and hostility, but eventually become at least tolerated as part of the American religious scene. Quakers and Baptists were viewed as dangerous or absurd in colonial days; Mormons and Adventists in the early national period; and Catholics and Jews at the turn of the century.

This pattern of intense problematization followed by accommodation has also been documented in the cases of the most well known "cults of the 70s" (the Moonies, Hare Krishnas, Scientologists and others).

This is not, however, a uniform pattern of the social adaptation of MRMs in America. There are also cases of MRMs that have exhibited a high degree of accommodation with their social environment throughout their life span. They have all the characteristics of MRMs as we understand them, yet they have never been significantly problematized. They have existed rather quietly in the margins of the American religious system, making few waves and eliciting little controversy and often little recognition from the press, public, or scholars alike. Some have been tiny or experienced declining memberships, while others have exhibited buoyant growth rates.

Among the cases that we examined in depth, the best illustration of this pattern is Nichiren Shoshu Buddhism in America. Even though it has some properties similar to the stigmatized "cults of the 70s" and a remarkable growth rate (claiming about 330,000 in 1983), it has been able to exist and prosper in a state of continuous high accommodation.

Similar cases of continuous high accommodation are not rare. Historically, one could point to the Amish, Mennonites, Swedenborgians, and Theosophists. American Baha'i, EKANKAR, atheist organizations, witchcraft groups and even the formally organized Church of Satan of Anton LaVey could serve as more contemporary examples. To get some sense of how common these patterns might be we turned to the *Encyclopedia of American Religions* which has cursory descriptions of 1,588 religious groups, probably the most comprehensive such survey. In addition to including descriptions of doctrines and histories, the encyclopedia has information about the existence and nature of external conflicts surrounding the religion. Using the most conservative research strategy, we ruled out the established churches and their smaller sectarian relatives that could be identified as belonging to an established "religious family" (e.g., the Liberty Baptist Fellowship, the Wesleyan Church). We ruled out sectarian relatives of the major denominations because it can be argued that they are not completely marginal—either in terms of size or doctrinal deviance. We were left with a set of 822 MRMs that were more likely to be *unambiguously* marginal in terms of all of the dimensions mentioned above (size, doctrinal eccentricity, cultural respectability, and power). Of these, 32 (about 4 percent) are noted to have had any external controversy or conflict (which we take as the most observable index of problematization). Even that small figure is a generous estimate: it includes, for example, those that have been involved in local land or zoning disputes, those whose internal difficulties led to external involvement, and those who may be or have been considered dangerous but have not been charged with any particular crime (e.g., Rastafarians).

While not definitive, we think this evidence means that high accommodation is far more common than high problematization, even among the most exotic MRMs. Like the public, scholars are likely to have more sustained interest in cases involving dramatic public controversies; our suspicion therefore is that others are underrepresented in both historical and sociological scholarly literatures.

A Theory of the Social Adaptation of MRMs in the United States

What factors shape the positive or negative social adaptation of an MRM within its social environment? How might these factors operate jointly? We address in turn: (1) religious doctrine, (2) movement structural attributes, (3) movement-society interaction processes, and (4) types of opposition and opposition coalitions. We have arranged these sequentially in what we argue to be their increasingly salient and concrete impacts on shaping the social adaptation outcomes of MRMs.

Religious Doctrine. By our definition, MRMs have beliefs that are deviant and unorthodox within their social context. As cases in point, consider the Shakers' belief in the divine incarnation in their leader Anne Lee and their advocacy of celibacy; the Mormon doctrines of continuing revelation, polygamy, and a hierarchy of living Saints; the Moonie belief that a Korean evangelist is the latest messiah sent by God after a long string of failures; the Hare Krishna belief that spiritual ennoblement is to be achieved by chanting praise to a Hindu deity; or the Scientology teaching that one is really a timeless spiritual being trapped within a human body who can be completely freed by an unorthodox therapeutic process. Even Roman Catholic doctrines, such as papal authority, priestly celibacy, and the veneration of Saints, were considered "deviant" in terms of the Protestant theological hegemony in nineteenth-century America.

Certainly religious beliefs are related to the social adaptation of MRMs. They *can* become powerful vehicles by which social conflicts between MRMs and their social environment are symbolized, but we argue that they do so largely when conflict develops for other reasons. As Moore has said of the Mormons, their behavior "gave importance to practices and beliefs that might with as much reason have been trivialized." The same might be said of the Shakers, Catholics, and "70s cults." The problem is that doctrine itself is relatively constant and does not change much as MRMs move from high problematization to accommodation (though its mode of public presentation does). Furthermore, as the cases of Nichiren Shoshu and contemporary Mormonism suggest, it is possible to maintain both unorthodox beliefs and high social accommodation. Religious belief may be directly related to other important things about MRMs, such as maintaining distinctiveness and mobilizing resources that are important for long-run viability, but as it relates to social adaptation, we concur with Pfeffer that

in every case the tension [between MRMs and society] is a function not of the group's theological beliefs, no matter how alien they might appear to be, but of positions or practices which tread upon strongly held national secular values. When by reason of change either in the group's position or in national secular norms, the threat disappears or becomes manageable, the legitimation of the group and its acceptance by the general community are practically automatic and generally simultaneous.

Notwithstanding this, some have argued that broad movement typologies based on doctrinal characteristics are related to the social adaptation of MRMs. Thus "refuge" MRMs are viewed as less controversial than "world-transforming / conversionist / revitalization" movements and "manipulationist" movements that "sell" metaphysical techniques to clients. We believe such typologies to be useful, but note that they are more about the implications of religious belief for social relations than about beliefs per se. There are empirical difficulties in applying broad typologies to specific cases. Intense problematization would seem to be found among diverse MRMs, from the Shakers and Hare Krishnas (partly refuge MRMs), to the Moonies and Mormons (conversionist MRMs), and Scientology and the Divine Light Movement (manipulationist MRMs). Furthermore, all types of movements have shown an ability to move into a more accommodative relation with their social environments. Among the large number of highly accommodated MRMs mentioned earlier one could find them also linked to diverse types of beliefs. It is true that religious beliefs do not exist in isolation but are composed of symbols that have implications for social practices and relationships. But the relationship between religious ideas themselves and the implications for social relations is a loose one; social relations are a more likely source of social opposition than the ideas themselves. In the case of problematization, MRMs are more likely to modify the implications of belief for social practice and social relations than the beliefs themselves. We suspect that, except for the opposition of competing religions, a focus on beliefs is largely a convenient and *post hoc* way of symbolizing opposition to groups that have become controversial.

Movement Structural Attributes. We argue that social practices and relationships of MRMs are more directly related to adaptive outcomes than beliefs. Before discussing those that we find to be most important, let us briefly mention those that are often discussed regarding particular MRMs but seem to be false leads in a general sense.

Considering a broad historical range of cases we do not think that structural characteristics such as size or the age or socioeconomic characteristics of members are very important for social adaptation. Size is particularly ambiguous. It is an aspect of marginality, though perhaps not the crucial one. It seems that both relatively accommodated and problematized groups have come in all sizes, from the tiny Shakers and Krishnas to the large and expanding Catholic and Mormon populations. Movement to higher accommodation can be connected to either continued growth or a decline in size. Similarly MRMs that have never been significantly problematized can be relatively small and stable (e.g., EKANKAR, Baha'i) or expansionary (e.g., Nichiren Shoshu). Some have argued that the youthfulness of the converts to the "70s cults" was a decisive factor in their problematization, yet such could not have been a cause in the case of Scientology, nor was it for most of the historic problematized MRMs. Some have argued that MRMs become problematized when they begin to recruit successfully among middle class (vs. marginal) populations, but again, this is not consistently so for a broader spectrum of cases. Nichiren Shoshu converts are by and large "middle-class." Catholics were most problematized when their socio-economic status was lowest, and evidence about the status of Mormon converts is mixed. In sum, we do not deny the relevance of these factors in particular cases, but they seem not to have a general impact.

Problematization is more likely if MRMs have associated with them forms of individual behavior or structural arrangements that are not conventional or normative; in a word, if they appear to be *deviant* in an American context. This can take the form of deviant sexuality or family arrangements (as in the celibacy and communalism of the Shakers, convents of nuns and celibacy of Catholic clergy, polygamy among Mormons, or widely publicized "arranged" mass marriages among Moonies). It can take the form of the mere appearance of people (as in the case of the "weird" attire, shaven heads, and public chanting of the Krishnas, or the perceived foreignness of early Catholic immigrants). It can take the form of unconventional economic communalism (as among the Shakers), "extreme" asceticism (as with the Krishnas), or centralized and authoritarian organizational arrangements (as with practically all of the movements we have surveyed). It can take the form of an "ethnic" or extranational connection (as in the cases of the Shakers, Moonies, Catholics, Krishnas, and Nichiren Shoshu). In varying degrees, all of these social attributes have the potential of calling into question the legitimacy of established values about, for example, "normal" heterosexual behavior and the nuclear family, individualism, capitalism, democracy, patriotism, and materialism.

Perhaps more significant than unorthodox values and behavior, however, is the unorthodox "bundling" of religious practice, economics, and politics, producing a "hallowed universe" in which a number of major institutional tasks are fulfilled in a distinctively religious way. Problematization is likely to result from any attempt to redraw the conventional "American" line between the "sacred" and "secular." Thus a MRM that also operates farms, restaurants, clinics, publishing houses, schools, and colleges run special risks. In this regard one could mention the fusion of religion and therapy in Scientology, the business and media enterprises of the Mormons, Moonies, and Krishnas, as well as the schools of Catholics, Krishnas, and the Amish. Other investigators have noted the vulnerabilities that come with such creative fusions of religious and other activities.

These creative "fusions" provide an additional liability, we argue, for two reasons: First, MRMs that conduct a myriad of activities and enterprises must not only "manage" popular prejudices about deviant beliefs and behavior, but also risk a high probability of "turf" encroachments on the territory of powerful established agencies and interest groups. This explains why one study of MRMs in a concrete community setting found them to be particularly disliked by many established mental health practitioners, some businesses, church leaders, counseling agencies, and college campus ministry organizations (Harper, 1982). Second, in such "protected empires" MRMs are likely to be perceived as substantially more outside government supervision and scrutiny than would be the case if they were not conducted under religious auspices. In contrast, similar operations conducted by established churches are more likely to be perceived as under the scope of societal regulation. Robbins suggests that in the contemporary situation such conflicts with the state result from the collisions between expanding "multifunctional" religious movements and the expanding regulatory powers of the agencies of the welfare state. While this is helpful in understanding the current situation, we note that conflicts between MRMs and agents of the state antedate the emergence of the welfare state in the United States and elsewhere.

Political deviance and intrusiveness is even more hazardous than ecological encroachments on the "turf" of economic, professional, and established religious agencies. MRMs have raised questions about their political loyalty by seeking special "exemptions" and denials of "civic" obligations (as in the pacifism of Shakers, Quakers, and Witnesses). Some have attempted to create a state within a state (e.g., the Mormons) and threatened the creation of a separate political party (as did Catholic Bishop Hughes in the New York legislature in 1841). Some have lobbied and conducted crusades in service of particular ends (e.g., the

"Save Nixon" and "anti-communist" crusades of the Moonies, and the Scientology schemes to monopolize nuclear weapons technology and "reform" mental health practices). Robbins has also emphasized the "sinister cultic state-within-a state" pattern as a source of difficulty for MRMs.

Significantly, the MRM among our cases that avoided problematization did not link the promotion of a highly unorthodox set of religious doctrines with deviant behavior, values, sexuality, or family arrangements. Nichiren Shoshu assiduously drew a "conventional" line between religious and secular affairs. Furthermore, members were not only to conform to social rules, but to be "winners" in the domains of social life, whether in jobs, school, or creating a harmonious household. Partisan controversy is avoided while Nichiren Shoshu portrays itself as a patriotic American movement, seeking to celebrate and revitalize liberty, achievement, and the American Dream.

As they moved toward accommodation, all highly problematized MRMs worked to modify the social practices and structural properties at the root of the controversy. Shakers, for example, willingly paid taxes (when they could have claimed religious exemption) and fees in lieu of military service, and they willingly modified "convenant agreements" concerning property with apostates, rather than be drawn into civil courts. After the nineteenth century, the Mormons disclaimed not only polygamy, but *formally* gave up theocracy, anticapitalist economic experiments, and participation in politics *as a church*. In short, Mormonism became more conventionally a religion and less a hybrid mixture of religion, economics, politics, and a family system. Fears of deviance and suspicion of disloyalty among Catholics were undercut by the increasing cultural assimilation of immigrants during the twentieth century. In the same period Catholic political behavior rarely challenged the conventional system or interests but instead became an important component *of* that polity. Similar changes have been noted regarding the 1970s cults. Most of the Unification Church's maturing members (young families with children) no longer live in communal centers, and it has created a "home church" category of membership for those wishing to lead conventional lives and participate only in worship services. The Unification Church claims to have given up high pressure and deceptive recruiting and has largely abandoned the public fundraising that made them so notorious in the 1970s. Finally, the Hare Krishnas have undertaken similar changes, shifting from street solicitation to their own economic enterprises, dressing in a conventional manner when appropriate, and establishing levels of membership to accommodate those unwilling to tolerate the ascetic regimen of their religious center.

In sum, we argue that in the United States the degree of social deviance has been more directly related to social adaptation outcomes than deviant doctrines, and that—as a general proposition—the greater the number of "deviant" properties and the higher the ecological intrusiveness, the more likely an MRM is to become problematized. Yet we also believe that, with the possible exception of threats to the sovereignty of the state, adroit movements can manage to "finesse" a number of these characteristics and avoid extreme problematization. We view them, in other words, as more powerful determinants than religious belief, yet still broader than the nature of interactional transactions between the MRM and powerful social agents.

Interactional Processes. Particular modes of interaction between an MRM and its social environment are more specifically related to adaptive outcomes than structural attributes. Indeed some of the potentially hazardous deviant and ecological attributes may be simply ignored when the quality of the interaction between the movement and powerful community agents is sufficiently positive and nonprovocative. On the other hand, when the interaction between the MRM and powerful agents in the social environment is negative, abrasive and provocative, the significance of characteristics that would otherwise be less important become amplified. Thus, similar to religious doctrines, the structural attributes of MRMs becomes more salient pretexts for their harassment following a history of rancorous and "ill-tempered" engagements between the movement and community agents.

By interaction processes we mean the myriad ways by which an MRM interacts with agents in its social environment, including collective "impression-management" or "face-work" strategies by which they attempt publicly to portray the movement and neutralize or deflect criticism. Such operating strategies and styles can be abrasive, conflictive, and seemingly paranoid. Deliberately or unwittingly, they can threaten or offend powerful community actors and agencies, as in the case of the nineteenth-century Mormons, the torturous confrontations between Scientology and government, or the occasional intemperate outbursts by Catholic clergy. In 1850, for example, Archbishop Hughes of New York City preached a widely circulated sermon in which he described

Protestantism as "effete, powerless, and dying" in the face of "Catholic truth," and explained that "everybody should know that our mission is to convert the world, including the inhabitants of the United States." As an even more dramatic example, in response to being denied the use of the Douay Bible in the public schools, Catholics in 1842 publicly burned a collection of King James Bibles. In these instances the movement *itself* may amplify its claims to religious exclusivity and graphically underline or display those very structural attributes (mentioned above) that have the potential to make them controversial. Such "abrasive behavior" may involve intermittent and unwitting bungling of things (as, we would argue, with the Moonies), but it may also take on a more systematic character, utilizing a "rhetoric of deviance" and a deliberately cultivated atmosphere of exclusion and oppression as strategies to legitimize charisma and build commitment to movement. Such seems to be the case with the organizational styles promulgated by the Mormons and Scientology.

On the other hand, a movement can cultivate a style of "accommodative flexibility," to use Snow's term, not only by abandoning those structural properties conducive to problematization (as in the case of the Mormons), but also by striving to "finesse" its structural liabilities through deliberately contrived "public relations," as well as more informal communicative "face work." It can seek to accumulate "idiosyncrasy credits" (as in the cases of twentieth-century Mormons, Catholicism or Nichiren Shoshu), portraying itself as "ultraconventional" in some respects while maintaining heterodoxy in others. It can seek to construct alliances with powerful established groups and agencies and to receive endorsements from notables, thereby gaining protection and some measure of social legitimacy. The Shakers, for example, utilized this strategy in the nineteenth century by inviting visits from notables such as Presidents Jackson and Monroe, Charles Dickens, James Fenimore Cooper, Nathaniel Hawthorne, Ralph Waldo Emerson, and Horace Greeley. They reported that the Shakers were being governed by admirable values (thrift, honesty, simplicity) and, at worst, were more archaic, quaint, or harmlessly peculiar than threatening.

Mormon leaders, in their shift to higher accommodation in the twentieth century usually sided with the American majority on the issues of the day (e.g., support for the Spanish American War, Progressive Era feminism, prohibition, both World Wars, and postwar anticommunism). On the few issues in which this was not the case (repeal of prohibition), the Church issued a simple statement of objection, being reluctant to lobby and raise the specter of theocratic intrusion into politics.

In spite of the contentious behavior of some Catholic leaders, most spokesmen worked hard to soothe popular passion. Given the increasing "Americanization" of the Catholic population, they gradually learned to "finesse" the strictures of both Vatican policy and popular prejudices to create a less problematic role for Catholicism in America. Similarly, Hare Krishna leaders in the 1980s have cultivated a significant supportive relationship with the Hindu immigrant community from India. They have aimed at shifting the movement more in line with the dominant culture and sought to portray it as a legitimate religious movement, rather than as a deviant group exploiting the American public.

Finally, an MRM can seek to avoid controversy by developing procedures to deal with or "appease" apostates, potential apostates, and those representing their interests (as in the case of the late nineteenth-century Shakers and the Unification Church's organizations for parents of members). This is particularly important because it is angry apostates and those representing their interests who usually provide the "atrocity tales" critical for mobilizing a popular base of countermovements such as nativism and the anticult movement of the 1970s. It is in this regard that we find Grove's account of the programmatic changes in Nichiren Shoshu to accommodate its "reluctant converts" theoretically interesting.

We have thus far emphasized the operating styles of MRMs, but in highly centralized movements the evidence compels us to emphasize the somewhat independent impact of the behavior and personality of particular MRM leaders. With the exception of American Catholicism, most were powerfully shaped by the personalities and predilections of their founders. Of the cases we examined, only Prabhupada of the Hare Krishnas seems not to have exacerbated the social tensions surrounding his movement by his own personal behavior. Indeed, we argue that for the rest it is impossible to account adequately for their adaptation histories without giving a prominent role to the aggressive, intolerant, abrasive, and often deliberately obnoxious behavior of Ann Lee, Joseph Smith, the Rev. Moon, or L. Ron Hubbard. Furthermore, we note that, with the exception of the Rev. Moon who still lives, moves toward real social accommodation became possible only after these powerful personalities were no longer on the scene.

In a hypothetical case we would argue in support of the thesis that if, for instance, Joseph Smith had been running the Oneida community (which was similar to the Shakers in its economic communism and perhaps *more* deviant in its sexual program), it would have become a shambles in short order. Instead—and in contrast to Shakerism—it enjoyed an almost fifty-year history of secure but not absolutely uncontentious existence under the leadership of the more politically astute Noyes. In the 1970s, the more accommodative social adaptation of *est* was significant, and its former Scientologist founder, Werner Erhard,

apparently . . . [learning] from the embattled position of Scientology in feuding with the psychiatric profession, and more recently with the FBI . . . was careful not to antagonize powerful interests. Thus *est* despite its being lumped in the public eye with other so-called "cults," has avoided major regulatory battles or lawsuits with the media which depleted the resources of groups like Scientology, Synanon, or the Unification Church.

It is perhaps true that the media always overemphasize the nefariousness of leaders, while portraying converts as only misled dupes. Still, because they are chief articulators and "impression-managers" in highly centralized structures, the independent impact of leaders' behavior cannot be ignored. If the outrageous behavior of leaders cannot be ignored in problematized movements, neither can the role of adroit leadership behavior in social accommodation (such as that of the successors of Ann Lee, or of George Williams in Nichiren Shoshu). Such skillful leadership is unlikely to figure so prominently in media accounts and scholarly attention.

In sum, for both historic and contemporary MRMs, those that were most "at risk" for becoming problematized were those that exhibited unconventional life-styles or structural properties and ecological intrusiveness, and in particular those that fused marital, economic, and political programs with religious doctrine. Furthermore, the likelihood of becoming problematized is heightened if there are negative, threatening, and provocative interaction styles between the MRM and powerful community actors and agencies, which may include conflict-amplifying behavior on the part of identifiable movement leaders.

Conversely, accommodation is facilitated by having few deviant social characteristics and a low degree of ecological intrusiveness. Typically this involves "untraconventionality" in some aspects that offset abilities of deviance in others. Narrowly "religious" rather than economic or political aspects are publicly emphasized, and to the extent consistent with maintaining its religious distinctiveness, the MRM takes on the social coloration of its environment. Furthermore, the interaction with powerful community actors and agencies is characterized by skill, adroitness, and "accommodative flexibility," including the ability to "finesse" volatile situations and the potentially provocative structural properties of the movement. The role of religious doctrine in the process of problematization seems to be as a set of convenient symbols to attack groups that become objects of contention for other reasons.

Movement Opposition and Oppositional Coalitions. Thus far we have focused on the characteristics of MRMs themselves that made them more or less "at risk" for problematization. But as a form of societal reaction, the process of problematization depends not only on the characteristics of the stigmatized groups but also on the nature and power of opposition, combinations, and coalitions mobilized against them. It is to this issue that we now turn. In doing so we will discuss the nature of such oppositional coalitions from the least to the most powerful, suggesting a crude sort of "metric" of positive and negative social adaptation outcomes.

High Accommodation. Many MRMs maintain high accommodation simply by low visibility. Sometimes this is carefully contrived low visibility in terms of the strategies of collective face work discussed above, but it also may be because they have simply not come to the attention of the media, politicians, scholars or other agents capable of shaping a public reality-construction regarding the nature of the movement. There is simply no opposition and no public definition of any kind. Indeed, this is the case for a large number of MRMs: of the 822 catalogued by Melton, only a small handful are generally familiar, and many are not, even to religious scholars. This is true not only for tiny groups, but also for some with more substantial followings (e.g., contemporary Spiritualism, Nichiren Shoshu, ECKANKAR, Baha'i, and the contemporary Satanist churches).

Accommodation (MRM defined as "peculiar"). In this reaction the MRM is widely, though perhaps vaguely, known to the public. Public criticism, if any, originates largely from representatives of established religious denominations. But these objections are likely to be discounted in public arenas as "special pleadings" over doctrinal issues. Most significant is the absence of opposition by powerful secular actors, such as professional groups, patriotic organizations, community neighbors and opinion leaders. The state may have an interest in regulating specific practices of the MRM (such as compulsory education regarding the Amish or the pacifism of the Jehovah's Witnesses), but such interest is not a surrogate for more generalized official opposition or oppression.

Such conflicts are typically mediated to satisfactory informal or judicial resolutions. Complaints of angry apostates are ineffective and attract little attention. Media portrayals and scholarly attention are either positive in character, or present the MRM as being "kooky" but benign. Emergent public definition views it as doctrinally deviant, but harmless. In spite of its unorthodox character, it may be viewed as representing some admirable values and perhaps as functional or adaptive for its adherents. This was the case for both the Moonies in the *early* 1970s, and for the Shakers in the late nineteenth century.

MRMs in this situation may neutralize potential opposition or shape public definition. Important ways of doing this include seeking alliances with respected groups, celebrity endorsements, modification of the most objectionable social practices, and a proactive campaign to produce a more positive public definition. Some MRMs in this state have extensive positive "connections" with established groups and agencies. Examples of such a "benign" accommodation include the Amish, Shakers after the 1840s, contemporary Jehovah's Witnesses, the Moonies and Transcendental Meditation before the mid-1970s, and the contemporary Mormons (if still understood as a MRM).

Problematization (popular opposition). The emergence of opposition by powerful secular interest groups (such as those mentioned above) is the most important foundation of problematization. Moral entrepreneurs and publicists emerge that help to mobilize popular opposition, define the MRM as threatening, and articulate grievances against it. An aggrieved category of apostates emerges that provides the basis for the manufacture of "atrocity tales." There emerges out of this a significant body of "anti-MRM" literature that intellectually articulates and justifies allegations against the group. These coalitions may oppose particular MRMs, or congeal into a more generalized countermovement that opposes many marginal groups (such as the nineteenth-century nativist movement and the anticult movement of the 1970s).

In this degree of problematization that we term popular opposition, MRMs face a powerful coalition of secular interest groups, religious opposition, media and scholarly hostility, and an active crusade against them led by apostates and those representing their interests. Emerging public definition constructs the MRM as not merely peculiar but as evil, malevolent, and threatening. The right to exist, taken for granted in the case of peculiar groups, becomes an issue. Officials are inevitably drawn into the controversy, but reluctantly and inconsistently so, sometimes siding with the opponents of the movement and sometimes protecting the movement from popular opposition. At this stage the overriding official interest is in managing the intensity of public conflict. MRMs can exist indefinitely in this state, though the costs of resource expenditure and lack of access to legitimacy may be quite high. Consequently at this stage there are adaptive maneuvers to neutralize such opposition; the most important of these were mentioned above. Examples of MRMs in a state of intense popular opposition include mid- and late nineteenth-century Catholicism, early nineteenth-century Shakers, and after the mid-1970s, the controversial "cults."

High Problemization (popular and official opposition). In this state the movement must contend with both the popular opposition coalition described above *and* general official opposition. Problematized MRMs in the nineteenth century provoked vigilantes, often because officials were unable or unwilling to protect them from mobs, or because existing law prevented officials from carrying out the "will of the people" against MRMs. Nevertheless, evidence suggests that there were frequent hostile statements made in public by elected officials as well as repressive legislation (in the Mormon case). Hostile political responses today take the form of punitive "investigations" and action by government regulatory agencies under the "cover" of official disinterest in religious matters.

Officials may act on behalf of popular opponents whom they represent, but state regulatory agencies have a whole host of interests of their own that they seek to protect, such as control of taxation, licensing, and legal compliance in general. Thus, in addition to FBI investigations and FDA "raids" on Scientology, there was an unsuccessful, decade-long effort by the IRS to deny religious tax-exempt status to the organization. The Rev. Moon was convicted for tax fraud, the State of California put the Worldwide Church of God into receivership upon being denied access to audit its books, and there was an attempt to apply the Fair Labor Standards Act to the Alamo Foundation.

Agents of the state may harass MRMs by maintaining covert surveillance, conducting hostile raids and inquiries, and selectively applying regulations to their activities. On rare occasions the state has proposed and passed legislation intended to change or control the behavior of particular groups. We emphasize that an occasional conflict between the state and an MRM is not particularly noteworthy. But the combination of powerful popular opposition *and* systematic state hostility produces the highest levels of problematization. The costs of fighting both popular opponents and a hostile state are quite high, particularly for movements that are marginal anyway. It is so expensive of a movement's resources and corrosive of its fragile legitimacy that this position cannot be maintained indefinitely without accommodative gestures by the MRM. Cases of MRMs in this position are, in our judgment, fairly rare, including nineteenth-century Mormonism, Scientology in the 1970s and 1980s, and to a lesser extent, the Unification Church and the Rajneesh movement.

Social Adaptation, Survival, and "Success" of MRMs

We have focused only on surviving MRMs. A more thorough historical accounting would show many more to have failed in the long term rather than survived, but not, we argue, *primarily* because of being problematized. From the cases we examined and from the 822 groups described in Melton's encyclopedia, we were unable to find many instances (2 of the 32 problematized groups) where there was credible evidence that a MRM failed *primarily* because of oppressive societal reaction. Mormons, probably the most intensely problematized MRM in American history, still survive, as does the Rajneesh movement after its denouement in Oregon.

Social adaptation seems not to be related to MRM success or survival in an immediate and obvious way. High problematization may make growth and survival more difficult by exacerbating the struggle of the MRM for legitimacy, resources, and converts. Yet such effects are ambiguous, since some of the most problematized religious groups survive robustly (Mormons, Roman Catholics, and Jews), while the powerful nineteenth century, nativist movement that opposed them exists only as remnants. Indeed, periods of high problematization and accommodation can be found in the histories of robustly growing and expansionaly movements, ones that seem small but stable over time as MRMs, and among those that dwindle into historical relics of once better times—having little social impact and highly doubtful long term prospects.

All this leads us to think critically about an accepted general- ization, namely that there is a curvilinear relationship between social tensions and movement viability. Or, stated another way, that movements succeed to the extent that they "maintain a medi- um level of tension with their surrounding environment; they are deviant, but not too deviant." The generalization may be true, but we think that the evidence about the relationship between social adaptation and movement viability is simply too complex to ac- cept it without much qualification.

What are some things that might qualify the relationship be- tween movement viability and social adaptation (or alternately, might simply be more important)? Though we cannot treat them here in any depth, several things come to mind. We have argued that religious doctrine or ideology in and of itself is not directly consequential in shaping social adaptation outcomes. We think it is more directly related to long-term movement viability if it maintains distinctiveness in a competitive religious environment, does not create barriers to membership, and provides personal incentives for collective action. The work of Snow and his col- leagues about ideological "frame alignment" processes and on- going movement mobilization seems particularly important in this regard. Put simply, in a voluntaristic environment, the char- acteristics of religious doctrine are important determinants of whether or not MRMs have a membership sufficient to operate and mobilize for survival or growth.

Besides doctrine and ideology, the ability to manage problems of internal organizational coherence and stability has long been recognized in the social movement literature as related to long- term viability. The ability of a movement to engineer an orderly transfer of authority between generations of leaders (or as Weber would have it, to "routinize charisma") and the ability to manage and enclose divisive schisms seem particularly relevant to move- ment survival and success. In sum, we argue that in the long run MRMs in America die more for their doctrinal characteristics or their inability to resolve organizational problems than for their external social adaptation, which by itself provides few clear clues about the long-term viability of movements.

Conclusion

We have provided a theoretical framework for ordering a wide range of observations about an important dimension of the interaction between MRMs and their social environments. In doing so we have extended the scope of societal reaction theory—conventionally applied to deviant behavior in small scale social settings—to understand the dynamics of social adaptation processes of MRMs. Our goal has been a theoretically coherent account of the factors and processes, arranged in increasing causal salience, that shape the adaptive outcomes of different movements and the same movements across time. Beyond this, we make two empirical contributions for understanding MRMs. First, MRM accommodation is historically far more common than contentious problematization. Second, movement social adaptation *per se*—either positive or negative—is of limited value for predicting the long range survival of MRMs.

As usual with theoretical explorations of broad topics, there are dangling questions and fertile ideas for future study. The most obvious of these is suggested above: to disentangle the complicated long-term temporal relationships between social adaptation and the causes of movement survival. Second, we would like to examine evidence from a broader range of cases than we have been able to consider (e.g., Jews, Quakers, Pentecostals). Third, our perspective has potential utility for exploring conflicts among religious groups closer to the doctrinal mainstream (e.g., the controversies surrounding historic or contemporary evangelicalism) or among marginal *political* movements (e.g., the Socialist Workers Party or Lyndon LaRouche's movement).

Finally, we are acutely aware that most of what we have said may be true only in a North American context. Some beginnings have been made in cross-national surveys of religious movements, mainly in West Europe and French Canada. Related to our concerns with social adaptation we find the research of Wallis most interesting, which finds differences in the societal reaction to MRMs between the United States and the United Kingdom related to differences in the sociolegal culture of the two nations (i.e., British official reaction is earlier and swifter and defuses the intensity of popular problematization). But the whole basket of questions and specifications about differential social adaptation of MRMs in various nations is an important agenda for future research.

V. CULTS AND THE MEDIA

EDITOR'S INTRODUCTION

The way certain religious cults and their activities are perceived is influenced largely by media coverage. To give one instance, the practice of Satanism has been widely written about and sensationalized on television. In the lead article of Section Five, Robin D. Perrin and Les Parrott III, in *Christianity Today*, discuss the Satanism phenomenon, specifically "satanic ritual abuse." Thousands of psychotherapy patients have claimed to be survivors of sexual abuse and torture that was carried out by satanic cults. But can any of these accounts, some in the form of best-selling books, be trusted? No solid evidence has been found to give credence to stories of a vast satanic network. The authors blame the obsession with satanism on the media.

The following article by Bob Cohn and David A. Kaplan, in *Newsweek*, examines the Santeria cult. Santeria began in Nigeria, made its way to Cuba by slave ships, and eventually arrived in Florida as refugees began fleeing Castro. The cult is said to have 70,000 members in southern Florida alone. What has drawn the interest of the media is the ritual sacrifice of animals, particularly chickens and goats, to appease the religion's god, *dodumare*. Animal rights activists have strongly objected to the practice, but the Santerians maintain the ritual as a First Amendment right.

In *Christian Century*, Anson Shupe reports on the shifting strategy of the Reverend Sun Myung Moon, leader of the Unification Church, since his parole from a federal prison in 1985 following his income tax fraud conviction. Although the impression in the 1970s was that the Unification Church possessed vast resources, Moon's American investments consisted largely of small down payments and extremely large mortgages. Always controversial, Moon was once a favorite media figure. Recently, he has conducted his life more quietly. His interests have shifted to Asia, where he has factories in Japan and South Korea, and investments in an auto parts factory in China. Finally, Peter Maas, in *The New Republic*, discusses Moon's new found interest in Russia, where he wants to establish 2,000 factories—and tap a vast new reservoir of potential Unification Church members.

MEMORIES OF SATANIC RITUAL ABUSE[1]

Sondra, a single woman in her early thirties, sought psychotherapy for depression and an eating disorder. But as her therapy progressed, she began to remember episodes of sexual abuse at the hands of her father. Upon further therapy, other memories emerged, recollections of ritualistic ceremonies involving the drinking of blood, animal and human sacrifice, cannibalistic feasting, and the worship of Satan. The memories seemed vivid and real.

Sondra's story would be chilling even if it were rare. But it is not. Thousands of patients now claim to be survivors of sexual abuse and torture carried out by satanic cults.

Amidst the sudden explosion of personal testimonies and public fear about Satanism in the eighties, hideous stories of a new kind of child abuse emerged—"satanic ritual abuse" (SRA). It refers to ritually performed physical, sexual, emotional, and spiritual abuse of children by members of satanic cults. Proponents of the reality of SRA believe that thousands of children each year are being victimized in satanic rituals involving cannibalism, sexual torture, incest, bestiality, and murder. Some report that more than 100,000 "adult survivors" have undergone therapy and uncovered previously repressed memories of these abuses.

The first case of SRA to confront the American public was that of Michelle Smith. Through therapy with her psychiatrist (and later husband), Lawrence Pazder, Smith claimed to discover previously repressed early childhood memories of debilitating physical and sexual abuse by a Satanist cult, which included some members of her family. The two described her therapeutic journey in the book *Michelle Remembers* (1980). According to Pazder, Smith's therapeutic experience culminated in an image of the triangular "tip of Satan's tail" emerging on Smith's neck. In 1980, Pazder

[1]Article by Robin D. Perrin and Les Parrott III, professors of Psychology, Seattle Pacific University. From *Christianity Today* Je 21 '93 18–23. Copyright © 1993 by Christianity Today. Reprinted with permission of the authors.

138									The Reference Shelf

presented a paper at a meeting of the American Psychiatric Association where he coined the term *satanic ritual abuse.*

Another popular book on satanic ritual abuse was Lauren Stratford's *Satan's Underground* (1988), allegedly a memoir of her involvement and escape from a Satanist cult. Like other SRA survivors, she described black masses, sexualized torture, as well as bearing three children who were sacrificed by the cult. Despite questions about the veracity of her story, Stratford continues to give seminars on the subject and has published two follow-up books.

The therapeutic community is divided over the accuracy of these repressed memories of SRA. The *Journal of Psychology and Theology* (JPT) devoted its entire Fall 1992 issue to the subject, with articles representing both sides of the debate. In one article, Ruth Shaffer and Louis Cozolino, both affiliated with Pepperdine University's Graduate School of Education and Psychology, describe a typical therapeutic scenario based on their survey of 20 self-described survivors of SRA: Most survivors do not enter therapy for SRA per se, but for "pre-awareness symptoms of severe depression, anxiety, or dissociation." The triggers for the SRA memories are usually a contemporary trauma or some "visual or auditory stimuli reminiscent of some aspect of the abuse." Typically, patients are female and begin therapy around age 27; the therapy lasts an average of seven years, involving several therapists (usually ending with a therapist who believes both in "the reality of the abuse" and "in [the survivors'] capacity to recover"). Repressed memories are rarely exposed all at once. "Many subjects progressed from memories of sexual abuse by acquaintances; to memories of sexual abuse by family members; and, finally, to memories of ritualistic victimization."

Shaffer and Cozolino note the remarkable consistency of the reports among survivors (even between adult and child victims). "All subjects reported witnessing the sacrificial murder of animals, infants, children, and/or adults. . . . The vast majority of subjects in this study reported severe and sadistic forms of sexual abuse by multiple perpetrators." They see the consistency in the reporting as a strong argument in favor of viewing these accounts as accurate.

Another common feature of the professional literature on SRA is a diagnosis of multiple personality disorder (MPD). According to James G. Friesen, a psychologist and adjunct professor at Fuller Graduate School of Psychology, in his popular book *Uncovering the*

Mystery of MPD (1991), children dissociate or split their personality to defend themselves from unrelieved trauma—usually sexual abuse. To complicate matters, Friesen notes in an article in JPT
that "demons can disguise themselves as personalities," especially
in cases of SRA. Thus the goals of therapy also include spiritual
warfare: "Alternate personalities need to be unified, and evil spirits need to be expelled."

Who Is Telling the Truth?

The testimony of survivors of Satanism provides compelling
evidence for its grisly existence. Experts have emerged to uncover
Satanism where we never knew to look. And much of their dig-
ging has been in the buried memories of SRA survivors. The question is whether the experts uncover Satanism or invent it. Can
these accounts be trusted?

One important factor to keep in mind is that we cannot dismiss these stories just because they sound outrageous or unbelievable. It was not too long ago that disturbing stories of sexual
abuse and incest were dismissed as fantasies. We did not allow
ourselves to believe, for example, that priests or pastors or parents could sexually abuse children. Now these horrors are well-
documented facts.

Also, the psychological community has established that adult
experiences can trigger repressed traumatic childhood memories
to emerge. Freud was the first to refer to this unconscious process
of burying painful psychic memories. Critics of the SRA theory,
however, maintain that some therapists, in their attempt to help
clients recreate horrifying experiences, may do little more than
provide an interpretive framework for a person who was abused
without a Satanist connection. Childhood memories are by nature
often vague and malleable.

Thus we must apply reason and biblical wisdom in determining whether there is a Satanist conspiracy to abuse and murder
children. We cannot merely accept at face value accounts provided
by self-proclaimed cult survivors, no matter how credible the witnesses may seem.

In *Michelle Remembers,* for example, Smith and Pazder provide
no corroborative evidence for their shocking account. Such evidence is impossible to obtain, they argue, because the cultists
"planted" disinformation, such as wrong dates, in Smith's memory; the Satanist cult is also said to have destroyed the evidence of

its crimes. Other experts go so far as to attribute to cults the ability
to create particular alternate personalities in victims. According
to Cozolino in another JPT article, coauthored with psychologist
Catherine Gould, these personalities perform specific functions
to protect the cult, such as "reporting information to the cult,
self-injuring if the cult injunctions are broken, and disrupting the
therapeutic process." Thus the survivors' accounts become, as
Friesen himself admits, "unverifiable," since any contingency can
be explained away as a cunning tactic by the cult to remain undis-
covered.

Still, some accounts have been discredited. After their investigation into the claims made by Lauren Stratford in *Satan's Underground,* Christian authors Gretchen Passantino, Bob Passantino,
and Jon Trott concluded in *Cornerstone* magazine that the entire
story was a "gruesome fantasy." Among the more outrageous
claims made by Stratford was that she was raped by Satanists and
used as a "breeder" of children for Satanist sacrifices. Although
Stratford claims to have had three children during her high
school and college years, the investigators could not find one
witness, nor did Stratford produce a witness. The Passantinos and
Trott did find people who knew Stratford during the years she
was allegedly pregnant, but all claimed emphatically that she was
never pregnant during that time. In fact, no evidence could be
found to support her claim that she had been involved with a
Satanist cult.

According to the *Cornerstone* article, Stratford's story was never
independently checked out and confirmed by talk shows on which
she appeared, such as "Geraldo," "The 700 Club," or even by her
publisher. They assumed its truth. After all, who could make up
such terrifying experiences? In all fairness it must be said, however,
her original publisher eventually did question the decision to pub-
lish her story and pulled the book from store shelves.

"What I have written in my books, I have written in the spirit
of truth," says Stratford in a response to these allegations appearing in *Bookstore Journal*. "If there are any errors, they are errors of
memory and not lies." Stratford's controversial book has now
been rereleased by a new publisher (Pelican), who claims the challenge to the book's credibility was "a compilation of circumstantial
evidence and petty character attacks."

Where Is the Evidence?

The lack of corroborative evidence cannot be ignored. A
seven-year study by the FBI concluded that there is "little or no

evidence of organized satanic conspiracies." FBI agent Kenneth Lanning, for example, confesses, "In 1983 when I first began to hear victims' stories of bizarre cults and human sacrifice, I tended to believe them. I had been dealing with bizarre, deviant behavior for many years and had long since realized that almost anything is possible. The idea that there are a few cunning, secretive individuals in positions of power somewhere in this country regularly killing a few people as part of some ritual or ceremony and getting away with it is certainly within the realm of possibility.

"But the number of alleged cases began to grow and grow. . . . We now have hundreds of victims alleging that thousands of offenders are murdering tens of thousands of people, and there is little or no corroborative evidence."

For nearly a decade, American law enforcement has been aggressively investigating the allegations of victims of ritualistic abuse. So far there is no evidence for the allegations of large-scale baby breeding, human sacrifice, and organized Satanist conspiracies.

As we watched the recent confrontation between federal agents and Branch Davidians in Waco, Texas, we could not help noticing that the press seemingly had little trouble locating defectors willing to provide details of the practices of David Koresh and his followers—this despite the fact that speaking out against Koresh could be dangerous. The availability of ex-Davidians is not necessarily surprising, as previous research has demonstrated that defection rates from deviant religions are quite high. Yet, when it comes to Satanism, a "megacult" supposedly so pervasive and sinister that the Branch Davidians pale in comparison, no one has stepped forward to lead us to an ongoing cult or to the remains of bodies used in human sacrifice, or to any other physical evidence that supports the stories of SRA.

Bob and Gretchen Passantino, who operate Answers in Action, a California-based Christian research organization, are impressed by the secrecy necessary to conceal such a widespread conspiracy. In a broad-based investigative report published in *Christian Research Journal*, they write, "Let's suppose there are 100,000 adult survivors [of SRA] who represent only a small subgroup of the conspiracy. They are the ones who were not killed; eventually escaped the cult's control; got into therapy; 'remembered' their abuse; and were then willing to tell others about it. . . . If we conservatively peg the average number of abusive events per survivor at fifty, that would give us 5,000,000 criminal events over the last fifty years in America alone. And not a shred of corroborative evidence?"

In defending themselves against their critics, advocates of the reality of SRA claim that the similarity of detail in survivor stories proves their accuracy. To assume that this is evidence, however, is to adopt "a naïve and simplistic model of contagion," according to Frank W. Putnam of the National Institute of Mental Health.

Putnam maintains that the ritualistic-abuse community is especially sensitive to rumors because victims and experts share the same educational networks. Experts on Satanism, talk-show hosts, movie makers, and news shows share the same stories. Given that experts are trained in what to look for, it is no wonder that survivor accounts are markedly similar, as were the internal communist revelations during the McCarthy era. The same could be said of the evidence for UFOs. Hundreds of people who claim to have been abducted by aliens give remarkably similar descriptions of the space ships and aliens.

Is Our Devil Too Big?

In order to fully understand SRA, we must realize how our culture has responded in the past to stories regarding the activity of Satanists. No matter how thin the evidence for Satanist stories, there seems to be a bias to believe them.

One example is the widely circulated story that an executive of Proctor and Gamble (P&G) appeared on a popular talk show (usually said to be "Donahue") and admitted he was a devil worshiper, and that much of P&G's profits went to the Church of Satan. Often the information is passed along as a flier giving the date of the broadcast, an address for how to write for a copy of the transcript of the telecast, and instructions to boycott Crest toothpaste, Ivory soap, and other P&G products. The details make the story seem more than rumor.

But it is all a lie. No one from P&G has ever appeared on "Donahue," and the company has no connections with the Church of Satan. Still, the pressure has been such that P&G felt compelled to remove its man-in-the-moon trademark from its products since some saw it as occult and thus confirmation of the company's link with Satanism. Regarding the "Donahue" story, Ann Jenemann Smith, public-relations supervisor at P&G, says, "The rumor just won't die. . . . We have publicized letters of support from Billy Graham, Jerry Falwell, and others to squelch the rumor, and we *still* average more than 20 calls every day about it."

Recently a similar rumor has been circulating, involving clothing designer Liz Claiborne's appearance on "Oprah" where she allegedly announced herself to be a Satanist. Inquiries to the show regarding a transcript are returned with a mass-produced postcard stating, in a tone that could best be described as annoyed, that Liz Claiborne has *never* appeared on "Oprah" or any other afternoon talk show.

Satanist conspiracy theories are not exclusive to major corporations. Numerous heinous crimes have been attributed to devil worshipers. For instance, a gruesome murder of a 39-year-old woman in Missoula, Montana, set off a chain of rumors that linked her death to a Satanist cult that was initiating a "high priesthood of Satan." Stories were told of animal mutilations, infant sacrifices, witches chanting in the woods, and satanic plots. In one report, the police received a hysterical call from a woman who claimed her neighbor was a member of the cult who killed the victim. She was sure it was true because he had been "sacrificing dogs." On investigation, the police learned the accused neighbor was a hunter who had hung several animal skins over his back fence to dry. Although the bizarre tales of satanic activity related to the murdered woman eventually ran their course, they made a lasting impact on many people in Missoula. The murder was later solved, and police found no evidence whatsoever that any Satanist cult was involved. Still, the local folklore is steeped in witchcraft, and the rumors live on in the minds of people with a will to believe.

In another example, a number of cattle mutilations, hundreds of miles apart in the plains states, were rumored to be the work of devil worshipers. The missing parts from some cattle were said to have been removed with "surgical precision." In some cases, the blood appeared to have been drained from the carcasses. Speculation about the perpetrators ran the gamut from UFOs to Bigfoot. But the most common story attributed the mutilations to Satanists. Official investigations, however, revealed that the gory deaths were the result of animal predators, such as coyotes.

The crescendo of reports on Satanism in Los Angeles led the city to create the Ritual Abuse Task Force. The task force, which has been controversial since its inception in 1988, recently received front-page headlines when several of its members charged Satanists with attempting to silence them by pumping the pesticide diazinon into the air-conditioning vents of their offices, homes, and cars. Despite the fact that diazinon poisoning is easy to detect, according to the epidemiologist assigned to the case,

none of the 43 supposed victims of the poisoning could provide
any evidence.

Who Is Behind the Panic?

These false reports and rumors should not lead us to conclude that there is no such thing as Satanism in America. In fact,
some people can be identified as Satanists. Furthermore, it is a
fact that crimes that were committed as part of Satanist rituals,
usually involving the mutilation of small animals, have been reported in the media.

Contemporary American Satanism can be traced to the late
1960s. The most celebrated Satanist church to emerge from the
decade was ex-carnival worker Anton LaVey's Church of Satan in
San Francisco. While the Church of Satan has never been numer-
ically significant (current estimates range from 2,000 to 5,000
active members), LaVey's church has attracted considerable media attention—especially his Satanist baptisms and weddings.
LaVey has made a point of being offensive in ways that have made
news and brought him undeserved attention. Other Satanist
churches include the Process, the Solar Lodge, and the Temple of
Set, but they, too, have attracted few followers. Still, in LaVey's
own *The Satanic Bible,* he claims that "Satanism *does not* advocate
rape, child molesting, sexual defilement of animals," and no organized Satanist church has ever been linked with practices associated with SRA.

Part of the blame for the obsession with Satanism must lie
with the media. While the "prestige press," such as network news
programs and national newspapers, has avoided explorations of
Satanism as hard news, more sensational shows like "Donahue"
and "Geraldo" have had a field day. With a broadcast every week-
day, such shows require up to 250 riveting topics each year. For TV
producers, the primary concern is ratings. And when it comes to
Satanism, people *do* watch. In 1988, a two-hour, prime-time Geraldo Rivera special, "Exposing Satan's Underground," set record
ratings of nearly 20 million people—the largest audience ever for
an NBC documentary. The drudgery involved in checking facts
works against the shows' goals of ratings and profits.

But TV is not the only culprit. One of the most celebrated
"survivors" of Satanism is Mike Warnke. His book *The Satan Seller*
was released in 1973 and promoted as revealing "the demonic
forces behind the fastest growing and most deadly occult religion

in the world." The book has reportedly sold 3 million copies. And for two decades, it has been cited by people inside and outside the Christian community to prove the existence of a large-scale Satanist conspiracy—that is, until recently. The self-professed ex-Satanist has been charged with fabricating his life story as a Satanist high priest. Significant evidence contradicting his alleged Satanist activity was revealed by Jon Trott and Mike Hertenstein in an article in *Cornerstone* magazine. College friends of Warnke's say his story of being a Satanist high priest does not line up with the life of their former buddy. Warnke has admitted to fabricating some details and to exaggerating, but he has thus far stuck to the rest of his story without countering any of the specific charges.

These and other stories have had an effect on what America thinks about this issue. A 1989 survey conducted by the Public Policy Laboratory of Texas A & M University reported that 80 percent of Texans believe Satanism is getting worse, and that it is something to worry about. Another study presented at the 1990 annual meeting of the Society for the Scientific Study of Religion revealed that more than 70 percent of today's churchgoers agree that Satanism is spreading rapidly, that it is becoming increasingly organized, and that it is a serious threat to society. Given this context, people have little trouble believing in an organized Satanist conspiracy to sacrifice and torture children.

Why Is It Happening?

If we are accurate in our skepticism of the extent of SRA, and of the Satanist scare generally, one very important question remains yet unanswered: How can so many well-meaning counselors, pastors, and individuals be wrong?

The answer begins with the recognition that counselors today, understanding that victim disclosures have historically been met with disbelief, are taught to listen to and accept victim accounts of abuse. More than at any time in human history, counselors are acutely aware of the symptoms, prevalence, and consequences of child physical and sexual abuse. Add to this sensitivity a societal fascination with Satanism, and distortions are bound to occur. In an interview on ABC's "Prime Time Live," Cory Hammond, a staff psychologist at the University of Utah Hospital and the "guru of SRA," stated, "Therapists shouldn't be responsible for providing evidence [of SRA]."

One explanation is that the concept of Satanism may provide

a ready explanatory grid for people trying to discover the source of their psychological problems. In a workshop entitled, "Errors in the Diagnosis and Treatment of MPD and SRA," psychologist Dane Ver Merris, of Pine Rest Christian Hospital in Grand Rapids, told the International Congress on Christian Counseling in Atlanta that many supposed survivors of SRA have psychological problems making them more susceptible to suggestions of having been ritualistically abused by Satanists.

It does not take much for imaginative individuals who have been abused to "recall" and believe that their abuse is directly connected to Satan. In coping with crisis, people tend to divide the world into simple categories—good and bad. In trying to understand confusing and horrific circumstances, any explanation can seem better than no explanation. After reading a book, viewing a show, or hearing a sermon, victims may discover a new hook on which to hang their traumatic experience. To objectify the cause of their pain can be an emotional release. This reasoning may explain, at least in part, the recent increase in victims who have "remembered" their satanic abuse. According to a report in *Charisma* magazine, even Lawrence Pazder, the psychiatrist who coined the term *satanic ritual abuse,* now sees SRA memories as more an expression of a deep level of violation caused by abusive family members than actual accounts of SRA.

How Do We Respond?

No one wants to minimize the trauma and terror victims suffer at the nefarious hands of Satanists or anyone else. No one wants to revictimize courageous survivors by not believing their horrific stories. Depraved people do evil things. And some people do perform gruesome acts of abuse, even acts that could be called ritualistic abuse.

Physical and sexual abuse, involving cultic activity or not, is plainly evil and influenced by Satan—whether or not it is done in his name. An individual's satanic abuse, real or imagined, should be taken seriously. The victim's pain and trauma is real and needs healing. We are called to shepherd the sheep, not shear them.

Still, we must avoid the danger Paul warns about in 2 Corinthians: "I am afraid that as the serpent deceived Eve by his cunning, your thoughts will be led astray from a sincere and pure devotion to Christ" (11:3). We have an obligation to listen to our Christian brothers and sisters, but we also have a scriptural obligation to evaluate what they say. We cannot fall victim to sloppy thinking or judgment based on a mixture of fallacies, nonevidence, and subjectivism. "He who chases fantasies lacks judgment" (Prov. 12:11). We must rely on careful Bible study, prayer, worship, and the fellowship and wisdom of other believers while we retain our commitment to compassion for the victims.

Some will argue that a reluctance to believe these accounts and a demand for evidence plays into the hands of Satan. They will argue that the Bible teaches us that Satan's influence is secretive and elusive. On this point, we agree (though one of the Devil's primary tools is confusion, and with that tactic he has been very much involved in the debate over SRA). Yet the burden of proof for disturbing stories of Satan's influence must lie with those who are making the claims. Extraordinary claims require evidence, and mere plausibility is not evidence.

Christians are by no means solely responsible for the Satanism scare. At the same time, we seem to have been especially willing to accept and spread the rumors. Christian author Jon Trott claims that when one looks at the "wads of Christian literature, tape, and airtime dedicated to alleged satanic cults, it is easy to conclude we've asked for it." We seem to have the will to believe and suffer little ethical pressure when we repeat rumors that may not be true. "There are a thousand hacking at the branches of evil," said Thoreau, "to one who is striking at the root."

A CHICKEN ON EVERY ALTAR?[2]

When Ernesto Pichardo leased a Hialeah, Fla., used-car lot in 1987 and announced plans for a church, the townsfolk mobilized. They signed petitions, they mobbed city hall, they cheered as legislators unanimously passed a string of ordinances aimed at driving Pichardo's parish out. "The neighborhood went ape," boasts Alden Tarte, who led the opposition. "He's not the kind of guy you'd want next door."

Fair enough (especially if you have a pet). Pichardo is no ordinary priest, and his ancient religion—Santería—is several tribu-

[2]Article by Bob Cohn and David A. Kaplan. From *Newsweek* 72 N 9 '92. Copyright © by Newsweek, Inc. Reprinted with permission.

taries off the mainstream. The religion, born in Nigeria, made its way to Cuba by slave ship and eventually into Florida by way of refugees fleeing Castro. Its congregants believe in sacrificing chickens, doves, turtles and goats to placate their god, Olodumare. In candlelit ceremonies to initiate new clergy, cure the sick and celebrate birth and death, a priest slits the animals' throats, drains the blood into clay pots and prepares the meat for eating. The 38-year-old Pichardo, a former Roman Catholic altar boy, says he's "lost count of how many thousands of animals I have killed." If he wants to continue the ritual, Pichardo will have to convince at least five justices of the U.S. Supreme Court this week that Hialeah's law violates the First Amendment's guarantee of the "free exercise" of religion.

Santería's practices, followed by 70,000 members in south Florida alone, may seem simply to pit the sensibilities of animal lovers against a fringe order of poultricidal zealots. But the dispute is a key test for the high court. The authors of the Bill of Rights sought to keep government out of church affairs. That freedom has never been absolute in American society—bans on Mormon polygamy or Pentecostal snake-handling have been upheld—but it has long enjoyed special protection.

Two years ago the Supreme Court undercut the safeguards that protected the practices of many religious minorities. The justices ruled that Oregon's anti-drug laws could be used to bar Native Americans from smoking peyote. In a sweeping 6-3 decision written by Justice Antonin Scalia, the court gave legislators vast discretion, as long as "prohibiting the exercise of religion . . . is not the object of [a law], but merely its incidental effect." In other words, the state could ban peyote smoking because it feared the effects of the drug, not to limit a religious practice. That hyperfine distinction worried Justice Sandra Day O'Connor, but she suggested few lawmakers "would be so naive as to enact a law directly prohibiting or burdening a religious practice as such."

Except, perhaps, the members of the Hialeah city council. They maintain that their law is not aimed at the Santería faith. "But if their religion demands sacrifice," says council president Salvatore D'Angelo, "they're going to have to adjust for the 21st century." Hialeah officials say their goal is to protect the health of residents who might be exposed to bloody carcasses that attract vermin, as well as to prevent unnecessary cruelty to animals. Two lower courts found these to be "compelling government interests"—enough to trump the Constitution—and ruled for the city.

Santería leaders argue that there is little to substantiate the health concerns. Their brief accuses the city of creating "after-the-fact rationalizations" to justify a law "enacted for the sole purpose of suppressing a religious practice." And it suggests that town leaders are hypocrites. "You can kill a turkey in your back-yard, put it on the table, say a prayer and serve it for Thanksgiving," says Pichardo. "But if we pray over the turkey, kill it, then eat it, we violated the law."

Steady Erosion

The Chicken Wars, as they've come to be known, offer the justices a chance to clarify their position on religious freedom—either to pull back from their widely criticized 1990 decision or to say they meant just what they said. More than a dozen religious groups have signed briefs supporting Santería. Says Steven McFarland, director of the Center For Law & Religious Freedom, "I hope the court hasn't lobotomized the free-exercise clause." Even the United States Catholic Conference, which filed a cautiously worded "Brief in Support of Neither Party," sides with Pichardo.

Critics charge that since the 1990 decision there has been a steady erosion of religious liberty. Federal courts have cited the peyote decision to allow increasing government incursions, for instance, permitting autopsies ordered on Orthodox Jews and Laotian Hmong over their families' religious objections. One federal court upheld the FBI's decision to fire an agent for refusing an assignment on religious grounds. An Ohio court wrote that after the 1990 ruling, the free-exercise clause is no more than a "puff of smoke."

Many religious groups are urging the court to scuttle the peyote ruling, not just throw out the Hialeah ordinances. For that to happen, new Justices David Souter and Clarence Thomas would have to sign on. So too would the court's putative moderates, O'Connor and Anthony Kennedy, who joined Scalia in 1990. It may come down to whether the court is more concerned about dismembered chickens or being accused of dismembering the Constitution. [Editor's note: In July of 1993 the Supreme Court ruled in favor of the Santería church.]

SUN MYUNG MOON'S AMERICAN DISAPPOINTMENT[3]

Sun Myung Moon, contender for New Age messiahship and self-proclaimed successor to Jesus of Nazareth, has continued to attract media attention since his parole from a federal prison in 1985 after serving time for income-tax evasion. Like a chameleon Moon changes quickly between the roles of religious prophet and corporate leader, performing spectacular mass marriage rites for thousands of his personally matched couples while shifting millions of dollars from one enterprise to another within his multinational conglomerate.

All the while he remains a visionary, confident that he can bring about a theocratic one-world government conforming to his own peculiar gnostic precepts. In his movement's writings, Moon is ever the Lord of the Second Advent, the messenger of God who must carry on where Jesus Christ failed, creating the millennial kingdom of God on earth.

But despite the publicity, the sensational weddings and the high economic profile, Moon's messianic adventure in the U.S. has largely been a bust. In fact, the Unification Church of America is severely curtailing its operations and reordering its priorities—largely for economic reasons. The U.S. component of the Holy Spirit Association for the Unification of World Christianity (the formal title of Moon's international organization) has never financially edged out of the red in any of its major enterprises. Across-the-board losses have continued despite infusions of more than $1 billion in cash and credits from Moon's East Asian sources during the 1980s.

As a result, in recent years Moon has decided to retrench the U.S. church and move many of its operations, personnel and resources back to the Orient. His prison experience no doubt soured Moon on pouring further resources into the U.S., where his movement continues to be an enormous financial drain. A shrewd businessperson, Moon is willing to cut his losses.

[3]Reprint of an article by Anson Shupe, professor of Sociology and Anthropology, Indiana/Purdue University. From *Christian Century* 107:764–766 Ag 22 '90. Copyright © 1990 by the Christian Century Foundation. Reprinted with permission.

Another problem has been his overwhelming lack of popular appeal. Opponents of Moon have always exaggerated his church's membership figures to highlight the threat of the movement. It is still not unusual to read in the press that the Unification Church has 10,000 or more full-time U.S. members and over 25,000 "associates." The more ludicrous estimates have stretched as high as 80,000 members. But internal church documents show clearly that even when its visibility was high, there were only about 2,000 committed Unification Church members in the U.S. Moon's support for a Watergate-beleaguered Richard Nixon, the federal investigation of Korean intelligence operations in the U.S., and Moon's conviction on charges of income-tax evasion did not help recruitment efforts. Defections, apostates burned out from the frantic pace of fund raising, and coercive and abductive deprogrammings kept membership low despite the church's notoriously active recruitment.

Thus the story of Moon's church is not really a rise-and-fall saga; the church never really rose as high as it appeared to. Yet during the 1970s and '80s Moon's Unification Church became for many of his critics the archetypal cult, seemingly wielding ominous influence in Washington, D.C., and gathering vast tax-exempt wealth while sweeping up the best and the brightest of America's youth through sometimes deceptive and intense conversion sessions. At Moon's beckoning these converts mobilized to canvass streets and airports for cash solicitations. His followers filled Yankee Stadium for a U.S. bicentennial celebration that pitched Moon's personal interpretation of civil religion, and they lobbied Richard Nixon in support of continued military aid to South Korea. The "Moonies" seemed an army to be dispatched for Moon's personal projects. Meanwhile, Moon resided in mansions while his true believers lived out of suitcases.

Since Moon's first missionaries entered the U.S. in 1959 and Moon himself arrived in 1971 to lead the faithful, his movement has stimulated controversy. His original goal was to incorporate a mass movement of North Americans into an international theocracy. His strategy (a brilliant innovation for spreading a new religion) was to create new economic enterprises staffed by members working at low wages.

The well-known practice of soliciting tax-exempt contributions from passers-by was actually intended only to provide start-up funds. Moon planned for his U.S. followers to operate more stable industries, as they did in South Korea and Japan; build an economic infrastructure for the church; and then use the U.S. as a springboard to missionize Europe.

But this plan never materialized. After only a few years of rapid growth in the early 1970s, Moon became viewed not as Korean-style Billy Graham but as a man who claimed to supersede Jesus and who redefined Christhood as an earthly status to which anyone with the right esoteric knowledge could aspire. There was a rush to expose and denounce him, and by early 1974, as Richard Nixon became entangled in Watergate, the prospects of Unificationism in the U.S. began to wane.

The reputed wealth of Moon's U.S. wing was in part the product of smoke and mirrors. During the 1970s it may have seemed as if Moon was on a spending spree, buying the former New Yorker Hotel, mansions and shares in banks, and starting up newspapers such as the conservative *Washington Times*, the *New York City Tribune* and the Spanish-language *Noticias del Mundo*. But these purchases were misleading. Most were financed with large inputs of church money transferred from South Korea and Japan, minimal cash downpayments and sizable mortgages. Moon's factories in Japan and South Korea, employing his followers at low wages and producing everything from government-contract firearms to ginseng tea and expensive marble vases, kept the cash flowing westward.

The teams of young fund raisers hawking flowers or peanuts or begging outright on the sidewalks helped raise needed money, but annual operating losses mounted. Moon's much ballyhooed purchases of fishing fleets and seafood canneries, for example, have produced almost no income. A $30 million factory to build fishing vessels never opened for a lack of expertise to run it. Moon's bold but forgettable venture into film—producing the movie *Inchon*, which glorified the Korean war—lost $60 million after being panned by critics and ignored by audiences. None of his newspapers has ever turned a profit. The *New York City Tribune*, to name just one, has had average losses of over $200,000 a month since its founding in 1975.

In late 1989 it became public that Moon was investing heavily in China, pulling out support for his failed investments in the U.S. Moon the businessperson had quietly negotiated a joint venture with the Chinese government to build an automobile-parts plant in Guangdong province, an area of China with a substantial Korean minority. Moon agreed to put up $10 million a year for 25 years and to keep the profits in China. In return he won the government's blessing to build churches and spread Unification doctrine in that country.

Ironically, some of Moon's auxiliary outreach enterprises, which were not originally central to his plan to convert millions of Americans, have turned out to be his main successes.

For example, for years he staged lavish conferences for scholars, clergy and other professionals, (some of which this author attended), hobnobbing with Nobel Prize winners and creating his own forum to give his theology a fair hearing. He converted no one. But such get-togethers—now sharply reduced in scale and frequency—spun off publishing ventures that have produced quality books and magazines with genuine intellectual value. Unificationist spokespersons now claim that this was really Moon's intention from the beginning; that is, his only goal was to create dialogue among intellectuals and restore thinking about ultimate values within science. Those who have studied the movement since its beginnings, however, contend this pattern has evolved by default.

During the mid-1970s Moon courted the Republican establishment, showing up at Washington prayer breakfasts and sending his followers to sing Christmas carols on the White House lawn when President Nixon lit the First Family's Christmas tree. Not long after, Moon, who was always eager to be photographed with political luminaries and to seek special decrees honoring his early evangelistic speaking tours from unknowing mayors and governors, suddenly found himself a social pariah in the shadow of Watergate.

But he began pumping a lot of money into newly formed groups such as the American Freedom Coalition (headed by the triumvirate of Moon's primary translator, Bo Hi Pak, and Christian Voice's Robert Grant and Gary Jarmine, with New Right fund-raising czar Richard Viguerie on the board of directors) and older ones such as the stridently anticommunist Conservative Action Foundation. The church also set up the International Security Council and recruited former Reagan administration officials, one a senior fellow at the conservative Heritage Foundation think tank. Moon's *Washington Times* evolved into an ideological clearinghouse for conservative news and opinion, a genuine alternative to the dominant (liberal) *Washington Post.* It is no small achievement that an ambitious foreign evangelist stalking unwitting celebrities to have his photograph taken with them has helped strengthen a network of right-wing writers and strategists.

On the religious side, Moon has made allies of such otherwise
unlikely prospects as fundamentalist Baptist Jerry Falwell and the
National Council of Churches' religious liberty director Dean Kelley, who joined Moon's appeal to the U.S. Supreme Court to
reconsider his 1982 conviction for tax fraud. Moon was accused
of using tax-exempt charitable donations to support his personal
lifestyle. Moon denied the charges, but the IRS claimed he knowingly evaded tax laws. Moon cried racism. Both Falwell and Kelley,
along with a *Who's Who* of American religion, including the Southern Christian Leadership Conference and the Church of Jesus
Christ of Latter-day Saints, countercharged that a Supreme
Court refusal to reconsider Moon's conviction was setting a dangerous precedent that could eventually abridge the separation of
church and state.

To religious leaders Moon plays on the underdog themes of
persecution and denial of First Amendment liberties, a pitch pal-
atable to both conservatives and liberals. To politicos he funds
right-wing groups concerned with family life, a strong national
defense and the perils of pornography. To liberals he offers the
opportunity for humanistic interreligious dialogue on subjects
such as world unity, peace and communication.

Moon has located the issues that resonate best with each con-
stituency. To each group he downplays or fails to mention his
messianic claims, his theocratic goals and his socialistic agenda. At
bottom Moon is no pluralist, but he plays well as one. He has
grown beyond issuing the bald predictions that used to alarm
rather than win potential allies, such as his declaration to his
followers in 1973: "The whole world is in my hand, and I will
conquer and subjugate the world," and "We must have an automatic theocracy in the world. So we cannot separate that political
field from the religious."

Moon knows that in the short-run his movement must build
on the mutual concerns of other groups. That he has been able to
overlap many of his interests with theirs to his benefit is a tribute
to his statecraft. No one really knows Moon's psyche. But his
"ecumenical" political and religious work is likely a ploy, not a
deeply held conviction. One need only read his speeches to his
supporters to see how quickly he drops any pretense of genuinely
ecumenical sentiments. What at first might seem to be an attempt
to break down sectarian and ideological barriers is really only a
pragmatic means to cultivate allies to combat current hostility.

In his discussions with both conservatives and liberals, politicos and Christians, Moon has succeeded in establishing a U.S. presence. But this successful networking will probably be the only gleanings from his otherwise failed U.S. experiment.

MOONSKIES[4]

On a pleasant autumn day last year, a select group of journalists was quietly ushered into a comfortable home in an exclusive neighborhood here, treated to a generous dinner, and given a tour of the house, including the private quarters, which only the closest of the host's friends have seen. The evening was filled with cordiality. Nobody asked questions about the things that landed the controversial host in so much trouble during the 1970s and 1980s—right-wing extremism, murky business dealings, mass weddings, allegations of religious brainwashing and political influence-peddling, and imprisonment for tax evasion. There was a reason for the journalists' self-restraint: they were Soviets whose visit to South Korea was paid for by the Unification Church. But the interview was nevertheless noteworthy: it was the Rev. Sun Myung Moon's first in at least a decade.

Moon is coming in from the cold war to smother his old foes with kindness and joint ventures. He seems to be embracing the heirs of Marx and Mao with nearly the same degree of passion he once unleashed against them. A few months after the Seoul interview, Moon, 70, made his first visit to the Soviet Union and met in the Kremlin with President Mikhail Gorbachev. The plump South Korean predicts a "moral and economic renaissance" for the Soviet Union, and promises to support it. Investments by his business empire are expected soon, possibly in a computer school and a hotel. The Unification Church movement already has become a key foreign investor in China. Firms linked to the church are pouring about $250 million into a massive car factory in Huizhou, in southern China, and the church is looking for at least $750 million more from outside investors to finish the plant and build

[4]Article by Peter Maas, Korean correspondent for *The Washington Post*. From *The New Republic*, 203:7–8+ N 9 '90. Copyright © 1990 by The New Republic. Reprinted with permission.

an industrial city and leisure resort at the site, about fifty miles from Hong Kong.

It wasn't long ago that Moon's shrill extremism and bizarre religious teachings were a source of some discomfort to conservatives. Bo Hi Pak, one of Moon's chief aides, once accused Democratic Representative Donald Fraser, who was investigating the Unification Church's alleged role in the Koreagate scandal (which involved payoffs by Park Tong Sun and other Koreans to members of Congress), of being "an enemy of [America] and all free nations" for hindering Moon's work and besmirching his reputation. In a recent interview at his Seoul office, Pak, now president of the church-controlled *Washington Times* newspaper, said calmly that the moment has come to "help the Soviets get out of the Communist system as quickly as possible so that they can join the world community of democracy."

Yet it's not just the rhetoric that's undergone changes as Moon and his stigmatized church try to enter the mainstream. The flower-sellers seeking a few dollars in airports are being replaced by businessmen putting together million-dollar deals in financial capitals. Reporters' questions are often answered rather than routinely ignored, though the church still refuses to talk about sensitive financial or religious activities. The church's money-losing foray into the U.S. print media is being overshadowed by quiet acquisitions in the cable television business.

The precise size of the global business controlled by Moon is unknown. The empire is not owned by Moon himself but by a web of Unification Church officials and members who funnel profits and investments to projects backed by Moon. Pak recently disclosed that a minimum of $100 million in profits and donations is annually put at Moon's disposal—and often the amount is much larger. The profits are the top of the business pyramid; the base is presumed to be enormous, though it reportedly rests on a foundation of debt.

An article by John B. Judis last year in *U.S. News & World Report* estimated that at least 335 companies worldwide are affiliated with the church, producing or selling a baffling array of goods: weapons, soft drinks, car parts, computers, machinery, clothing, and fish, to name a few. When Americans visit health food stores to buy Korean ginseng, chances are they will be purchasing herbal roots grown and marketed by Moon's Ilhwa firm. Japanese and American office workers might be using computers produced by Wacom, a Unification firm in Tokyo, which are sold under several Japanese brand names, including Mitsubishi. East Germany may be rebuilt in part with some heavy machinery produced by a Moon business in West Germany.

The Unification Church's unexpected push into the Soviet Union remains in its infancy, with goals being articulated more quickly than actual projects. Church officials say Moon wants to help establish 2,000 factories in the formerly evil empire, either through church firms or by aiding Soviet entrepreneurs. "We're trying to encourage capital investment and joint ventures that will keep the economy from going belly-up," says Larry Moffitt, executive director of the church's World Media Association. He said Moon is prepared to commit "tremendous resources" to the Soviet Union, though he would not say how much. In October Pak took to Moscow a delegation of businessmen from Japan, the United States, and South Korea interested in investing in the Soviet Union. Many of them are church members. While there, Pak handed Raisa Gorbachev a $100,000 check as a donation for a cultural foundation she heads.

Aside from the computer school and hotel project in Moscow, officials say that the church might also be interested in helping Soviet road construction to complete one of Moon's fantastic pet projects—an "international peace highway" across the world. It's unclear whether anything will happen soon. The chaos in Moscow makes it difficult for any investor, even an enthusiastic corps of Moonies, to strike deals.

The church also has begun a process of political cross-fertilization by sponsoring a trip to the United States by about 380 Soviet students and professors for lectures about America and religion. The seminars, held in July and August, were organized by the Collegiate Association for the Research of Principles (CARP), the right-wing student group founded by church members. "The Soviet Union is opening up, and there is a lot of junk coming in there—immorality and drugs," said Bjorn Ottosson, CARP's assistant director for the Soviet project. "We want the Soviets to see what has happened in America to prevent it from happening in the Soviet Union."

The financial stakes are highest in China. The Chinese car firm, Panda Motors Corporation, was negotiated and agreed on in the days before the Chinese government took a bloody turn in June 1989. Moon is now in the awkward position of dealing with a leadership that has shed its reformist political clothing while instituting an austerity program. The global car market has become

more competitive than ever for established firms; an inex-
perienced odd couple like Moon's church and China's government faces an uphill battle. According to Pak, the car factory is to
reach an annual output of 300,000 units for export by 1995. The
vehicles will be called Pandas and reportedly will be based on the
Chevrolet Chevette, for which Panda Motors has bought design
and production equipment from General Motors.

Moon's resurrection is hardly a welcome event for his many
critics, who have accused him of brainwashing America's children
in an attempt to rule the world by establishing a right-wing corporate theocracy. Whatever his political motivations, his religion has
hardly taken hold in his own homeland of South Korea, where his
critics say membership is a humble 50,000. The membership ros-
ter in the United States appears to be even smaller than in South
Korea. But the virgin territory in the Soviet Union and China is
tempting for the church. And unlike other religions seeking to
gain converts among the godless masses, the Unification Church
can use its business empire to open many doors.

Talk of recruitment is quickly dampened by Pak. "Many
people suspect that Reverend Moon has ulterior motives," he
said. "I will absolutely deny that allegation." For now the religious
goals and activities seem to be given a low profile; an aggressive
recruitment program would draw attention to Moon's religious
goals, upset the political leadership in China and the Soviet
Union, and possibly scare investors away. Even so, the church is
not standing by idly as new evangelical frontiers open up. Several
members said the church is organizing a quiet network of underground missionaries and believers in these countries. When
Moon was in Moscow, he gave a speech titled "True Unification
and One World," which was more religious than political, touch-
ing on the main themes of his breakaway theology. Church officials confirm that they are trying to set up an office in Moscow,
but they insist that this initial presence will focus on business.

It would be easy to dismiss Moon as a mere cult leader—and
one who has been widely discredited. But he has survived and, in
some modest ways, overcome adversity. The move into the Communist and former Communist world is just another example of
his adaptability. His ever-loyal followers may think he succeeds
because he's the Messiah. But shrewd businessman and charismatic leader that he is, Moon doesn't seem to need God's help.

BIBLIOGRAPHY

An asterisk (*) preceding a reference indicates that the material or part of it has been reprinted in this book.

BOOKS AND PAMPHLETS

Adler, Margot. Drawing down the moon: witches, druids, goddess-worshippers, and other pagans in America today. Beacon Press. '86.

Allen, Steve. Beloved son: a story of the Jesus cults. Bobbs-Merrill. '82.

Andres, Rachel and Lane, James R. Cults & consequences. Jewish Federation Council of Greater Los Angeles. '88.

Appel, Willa. Cults in America. Holt, Rinehart & Winston. '83.

Atack, Jon. A piece of blue sky—Scientology, Dianetics, and L. Ron Hubbard exposed. Carol. '90.

Barker, Eileen. The making of a Moonie: choice or brainwashing? Blackwell. '84.

Beckford, James A. Cult controversies: the social response to the new religious movements. Tavistock. '85.

Bednarowski, Mary F. New religions and theological imagination in America. Indiana University Press. '89.

Biermans, John T. The odyssey of new religious movements. E. Mellen Press. '86.

Breaut, Marc. Inside the cult: a member's exclusive chilling account of madness and depravity in David Koresh. Dutton. '93.

Bromley, David G. Strange gods: the great American cult scare. Beacon. '81.

Bussell, Harold. Unholy devotion: why cults lure Christians. Zondervan. '83.

Chidester, David. Salvation & suicide: an interpretation of Jim Jones, the People's Temple, & Jonestown. Indiana University Press. '88.

Choquette, Diane. New religious movements in the United States and Canada. Greenwood. '85.

Chryssidis, George. The advent of Sun Myung Moon. St. Martin's Press. '91.

Collins, John J. The cult experience. Thomas. '91.

Colvin, Rod. Evil Harvest: the shocking true story of cult murder in the American heartland. Bantam. '92.

Committee on Psychiatry and Religion. Leaders and followers: a psychiatric perspective on religious cults. American Psychiatric Press. '92.

Corydon, Bent & Hubbard, L. Ron, Jr. L. Ron Hubbard: messiah or madman? Lyle Stuart. '87.

D'Angelo, Louise. The Exposing of a cult. Maryheart Crusaders. '93.

Davis, Deborah B. The children of God: the inside story. Zondervan. '84.

Dean, Roger A. Moonies: a psychological analysis of the Unification Church. Garland. '92.

Deikman, Arthur. The wrong way home: uncovering the patterns of cult behavior in American society. Beacon. '90.

Dumont, Larry C., Jr. & Altesman, Richard I. A parent's guide to teens & cults. PIA Press. '89.

Durst, Mose. To bigotry, no sanction: Reverend Sun Myung Moon and the Unification Church. Regnery. '84.

Eisenberg, Gary, ed. Smashing the idols: a Jewish inquiry into the cult phenomenon. Aronson. '88.

Ellwood, Robert S. & Partin, Harry. Religious & spiritual groups in modern America. Prentice-Hall. '88.

Endleman, Robert. Jonestown & the Manson family—race, sexuality & collective madness. Psyche Press. '93.

Enroth, Ronald, et al. A guide to cults & new religions. InterVarsity. '83.

————. and Melton, J. Gordon. Why cults succeed where the church fails. Brethren. '85.

Feinsod, Ethan. Awake in a nightmare: Jonestown, the only eyewitness account. Norton. '81.

Galanter, Marc. Cults: faith, healing, and coercion. Oxford University Press. '89.

Gonzalez-Wippler, Migene. Santeria—the religion: a legacy of faith, rites, and magic. Harmony. '89.

Hassan, Steven. Combatting cult mind control. Park Street Press. '90.

Hexham, Irving & Poewe, Karla. Understanding cults and new religions. W. B. Eerdmans. '86.

Hicks, Robert D. In pursuit of satan: the police and the occult. Prometheus. '91.

Hubner, John & Gruson, Lindsey. Monkey on a stick: murder, madness and the Hari Krishnas. Harcourt Brace Jovanovich. '88.

Hunt, Dave. The cult explosion. Harvest House. '80.

Isser, Natalie & Schwartz, L. The history of conversion and contemporary cults. P. Lang. '88.

Kaslow, Florence and Sussman, Marvin B. Cults and the family. Wadsworth. '82.

Keiser, Thomas W. & Keiser, Jacqueline. The anatomy of illusion: religious cults & destructive persuasion. Thomas. '87.

Klineman, George. The cult that died: the tragedy of Jim Jones and the People's Temple. Putnam. '80.

Kyle, Richard. The religious fringe: a history of alternative religions in America. InterVarsity. '93.

Lane, David C. Understanding cults & spiritual movements. Del Mar. '89.

Larson, Bob. Larson's new book of cults. Tyndale. '89.

Lewis, I. M. Religion in context: cults & charisma. Cambridge University Press. '86.

Lind, Mary Ann. From Nirvana to the new age. Baker. '91.

Linedecker, Clifford L. Massacre at Waco: the shocking true story of cult leader David Koresh & the Branch Davidians. St. Martin's Press. '93.

MacGregor, Lorri. Coping with cults: practical insights for concerned Christians. Harvest House. '92.

Mac Hovee, Frank J. Cults & personality. Thomas. '89.

Madigan, Tim. See no evil: blind devotion. Summit. '93.

Marrs, Texe. New age cults & religions. Living Truth. '90.

Martin, Paul. Cult-proofing your kids. Zondervan. '93.

Martin, Walter. The new cults. Vision House. '80.

———. The kingdom of the cults. Bethany. '85.

———. The new age cult. Bethany. '89.

Mather, George A. & Nichols, Larry A. Dictionary of cults, sects, religions, and the occult. Zondervan. '93.

McDowell, Josh & Stewart, Don. The deceivers: what cults believe, how they lure followers. Nelson. '92.

*Melton, J. Gordon. The cult experience. Pilgrim. '82.

———. Biographical dictionary of American cult & sect leaders. Garland. '86.

———. Encyclopedic Handbook of cults in America. Garland. '92.

———. New age encyclopedia. Gale. '90.

———. The Unification Church: view from the outside. Garland. '90.

———. The cult controversy: a guide to sources. Garland. '92.

———. ed. People's Temple and Jim Jones: broadening our perspective. Garland. '90.

———. ed. Cults & new religions: sources for the study of nonconventional religious groups in nineteenth & twentieth-century America. 22 vols. Garland. '92.

Mickler, Michael. The Unification Church in America: a bibliography and research guide. Garland. '87.

———. A history of the Unification Church. Garland. '93.

Miller, Russell. Bare faced messiah: the true story of L. Ron Hubbard. Henry Holt. '88.

Miller, Timothy, ed. When prophets die: the post charismatic fate of new religious movements. State University of New York Press. '91.

Milne, Hugh. Bhagwan: the god that failed. St. Martin's Press. '87.

Mosatche, Harriet. Searching: practice & beliefs of the religious cults & human potential movements. State University of New York Press. '91.

Murphy, Joseph M. Santeria: an African religion in America. Beacon. '88.

Naipaul, Shiva. Journey to nowhere: a new world tragedy. Simon & Schuster. '81.

Parker, Pat. Jonestown & other madness. Firebrand. '85.

Pavlos, Andrew J. The cult experience. Greenwood. '82.

Penton, James A. Apocalypse delayed: the story of Jehovah's Witnesses. University of Toronto Press. '85.

Perez y Mena, Andrew Isidoro. Speaking with the dead: development of Afro-Latin religion among Puerto Ricans in the United States. AMS Press. '91.

Plumb, Lawrence. A critique of the human potential movement. Garland. '93.

Porterfield, Kay M. Blind faith: recognizing & recovering from dysfunctional religious groups. CompCare. '93.

Raschke, Carl A. Painted black: from drug killings to heavy metal: the alarming true story of how Satanism is terrorizing our communities. Harper & Row. '90.

Reitman, Tim. Raven: the untold story of the Rev. Jim Jones and his people. Dutton. '82.

Reston, James. Our father who art in hell. Times Books. '81.

Richardson, James, et al, eds. The Satanism scare. De Gruyter. '91.

Robbins, Thomas. Cults, converts and charisma: the sociology of new religious movements. Sage. '88.

————. et al, eds. Cults, culture, and the law: perspectives on new religious movements. Scholars Press. '85.

Ross, Joan C. & Langone, Michael D. Cults: what parents should know. Carol. '89.

Sakheim, David K. & Devine, Susan E. Out of darkness: exploring satanism and ritual abuse. Lexington. '92.

Saliba, John A. Psychiatry and the cults: an annotated bibliography. Garland. '87.

————. Social science and the cults: an annotated bibliography. Garland. '90.

Shupe, Anson D. The anti-cult movement in America: a bibliography and historical survey. Garland. '84.

Storm, Rachel. In search of heaven on earth: the history of the new age. Bloomsbury. '93.

Streiker, Lowell D. New age comes to main street. Abingdon. '90.

Strelley, Kate. The ultimate game: the rise and fall of Bhagwan Shree Rajneesh. Harper & Row. '87.

Tucker, Ruth A. Another gospel: alternative religions and the new age movement. Zondervan. '89.

Turner, Karla. Into the fringe. Berkley. '92.

Wallis, Roy. The elementary forms of the new religious life. Routledge & Kegan Paul. '84.

Watson, William. Concise dictionary of cults & religions. Moody. '91.

Weber, Bert. Rajneeshpuram: who were its people? Webb. '90.

Wilson, Bryan R. The social dimensions of sectarianism: sects and new religious movements in contemporary society. Oxford University Press. '90.

Worden, Kenneth. The children of Jonestown. McGraw-Hill. '81.

Yanoff, Morris. Where is Joey? Lost among the Hari Krishnas. Swallow. '81.

ADDITIONAL PERIODICAL ARTICLES WITH ABSTRACTS

For those who wish to read more widely on the subject of religious cults in America, this section contains abstracts of additional articles that bear on the topic. Readers who require a comprehensive list of materials are advised to consult the *Reader's Guide to Periodical Literature* and other Wilson indexes.

Equal sights for religion. *America* 17–24 J1 '93

Two recent Supreme Court decisions reaffirmed longstanding doctrines that oppose religious persecution and forbid discrimination against religious speech. In one decision, the Court ruled that a set of ordinances in Hialeah, Florida, that forbade the ritual sacrifice of animals amounted to a persecution of the practices of the Santeria religion. The other decision involved a Long Island, New York, evangelical church, Lamb's Chapel, which was prevented from using the facilities of a public school because of a state statute that required public schools to discriminate against religion in the rental of their facilities. The Court ruled that the statute violates freedom of speech if it is applied to prevent the presentation of religious viewpoints on topics that the public schools allow groups to discuss from a nonreligious point of view.

Adventists disavow Waco cult. *The Christian Century* 110:285–6
Mr 17 '93

In a statement issued from its headquarters in Silver Spring, Maryland,
the Seventh-Day Adventist Church denied any connection with the
Branch Davidians, a violent cult that began more than 60 years ago as a
group of disaffected Adventists. Led by David Koresh, who claims to be
Jesus Christ, the Davidians recently engaged in a shootout with federal
agents at the cult's compound near Waco, Texas. The Adventist statement
reports that Koresh was a member of the Seventh-Day Adventist Church
for a period but was disfellowshipped from a Texas church in 1981.
Although none of the Davidians is believed to be Adventist, the cult has
targeted Adventists in its evangelical efforts. The size, history, and traditions of the Seventh-Day Adventist Church and the Branch Davidians are
discussed.

Drawing down the moon. Dave Bass *Christianity Today* 35:14–19
Ap 29 '91

Many Europeans and North Americans are turning to a spiritual and
philosophical movement loosely termed neopaganism. Neopagans may
include modern druids, participants in witchcraft, voodoo practitioners,
scientists who worship a mysterious life force, or free spirits who fashion
an amalgam of esoteric beliefs. They object to religions that insist on one
god, and they complain about people's association of neopaganism with
Satanism, which they disown. Recent estimates indicate that there were
nearly 100,000 practicing pagans in the United States as of 1989, and the
numbers are growing. Pagans worship in a circle, coven, or grove that is
headed by a priest or priestess and that meets outdoors twice monthly and
on eight pagan holidays. They believe in fate, worship the natural world,
stress ritual, and have an antipathy toward the Judeo-Christian faith.

New Kingdoms for the cults. Joe Maxwell *Christianity Today*
36:37–40 Ja 13 '92

Aberrant Christian groups, sects, and Eastern religions are mounting
organized campaigns in Eastern Europe and the Soviet Union. Like
Christian evangelists, missionaries for these groups are succeeding in attracting converts, and some are seeking acceptance by newly established
governments. Soviet leader Mikhail Gorbachev, for example, has in the
last year met with Sun Myung Moon, leader of the Unification Church;
Daisaku Ikeda, leader of a large Buddhist sect; and Sri Chinmoy, a New
Age guru popular in America. Some evangelical missionaries are frus-
trated by such groups. According to Charles Spine of Campus Crusade in
the Soviet Union, meetings have been invaded by Jehovah's Witnesses;
Mormons are building churches and deceiving would-be Christians;
and Hare Krishnas appear in every metro station in Moscow and St.
Petersburg. In the opinion of Paul Carden of the Christian Research

Institute, Eastern Europeans are all but defenseless against this "cult invasion."

Scientologists sue critics. *Christianity Today* 37:53+ F 8 '93

The Church of Scientology has leveled a barrage of lawsuits against the Cult Awareness Network (CAN), most of which charge the anticult group with religious discrimination for not allowing Scientologists to join. Mary Anne Ahmand, director of public affairs for the Church of Scientology of Illinois, contends that CAN, which was founded after the 1978 Jonestown mass suicide to promote public awareness of "destructive cults," has strayed from its original purpose by spreading defamatory information about Scientology. CAN, which believes that the lawsuits are part of a plan to destroy their organization from within, recently won several victories in federal and state courts. In addition, CAN executive director Cynthia Kisser has filed a personal suit against several publications and individuals connected to the Church of Scientology, the Unification Church, and the organization of Lyndon LaRouche.

Moonstruck in Connecticut. Linda Murray Green *Christianity Today* 37:54 Je 21 '93

An alliance of Bridgeport, Connecticut-area residents is challenging the Unification Church's role in the University of Bridgeport's rescue. Last spring, UB accepted a $50 million loan and grant package from the Professors of World Peace Academy (PWPA), a 10,000-member alliance of academics founded by Sun Myung Moon. In exchange, the PWPA received control of the university's board of trustees. Plaintiffs—including UB alumni, former trustees, and donors—have filed a suit that questions the PWPA's operation of a university with a nonsectarian charter. Although the PWPA is independent by charter, 90 percent of its money comes from the Unification Church. The plaintiffs' lawyer says that the suit's main goal is to reorganize the board of trustees, which is now 60 percent PWPA-controlled.

Nyet to religious liberty. *Christianity Today* 37:44 Ag 16 '93

On July 14, the Russian parliament voted to amend the 1990 Law on Freedom of Conscience and Religious Organizations. The vote effectively prohibits independent activities of foreign religious organizations, their representatives, and individual religious workers who are not Russian Federation citizens, and it requires foreign religious groups to affiliate themselves with Russian organizations or churches or to obtain state accreditation. Protestant church leaders in Russia and U.S. politicians have called on President Boris Yeltsin to veto the bill. If he does sign the bill, he risks losing Western aid, but if he vetoes it, he will offend the 60 million-member Russian Orthodox Church, which has become concerned with the proselytizing efforts of such groups as the Hare Krishnas, the Mormons, and the Unification Church over the last 5 years.

The search for scapegoat deviants. Jeffry S. Victor, *The Humanist* 52:10–13 S/O '92

An article adapted from Rumors of Evil. The recent panic over satanic cults in America illustrates the process by which social preoccupations give rise to invented scapegoats. When societies are troubled by internal conflict, external threats, or disputes over moral values, they often construct sinister, deviant stereotypes that are then attributed to a particular group of people. These perceived deviants take the blame for the society's problems, and other tensions and hostilities are eased as people close ranks against the scapegoats. With its emphasis on allegations of ritual child abuse, teen suicide, and other threats to young people, the satanic cult scare may be a projection of society-wide parental guilt and ambivalence toward children. This imaginary menace also promotes cooperation among some fundamentalist Protestants, conservative Catholics, secular feminists, children's advocates, police officers, social workers, and psychotherapists.

The ant hill kids. *Maclean's* 106:4, 18–20+ F 8 '93

A cover story examines cults. During a period of 11 years, Roch Theriault, a native of Riviere-du-Moulin, Quebec, and a self-styled prophet, headed a cult known as the Ant Hill Kids. The cult, which was first located on Quebec's Gaspe Peninsula and later moved to Ontario, caused the deaths of at least 2 members, left several others permanently maimed, and inflicted severe emotional scars on many of the 25 children whom Theriault fathered with 8 of his concubines. Theriault, who was convicted in 1989 for hacking off one cult member's arm with a meat cleaver, is currently serving a life sentence for the murder of another member. An article discusses reasons why cults attract people, and an editorial comments on the influence that Theriault continues to exert on his followers.

Faith in firearms. Christopher Wood, *Maclean's* 106:28+ Mr 22 '93

The standoff between authorities and the heavily armed Branch Davidian religious sect near Waco, Texas, has resulted in increased support for gun-law reform. On February 28, agents of the U.S. Bureau of Alcohol, Tobacco and Firearms launched an unsuccessful raid against self-proclaimed prophet David Koresh's Branch Davidian sect, which was suspected to possess an arsenal of assault weapons, explosives, hand grenades, and at least one .50-caliber weapon capable of firing rounds designed to pierce light armor. The botched raid resulted in the deaths of 4 agents; subsequent negotiations with Koresh and more than 100 followers became bogged down. The conflict apparently unleashed growing public support for such gun-reform proposals as the Brady Bill and various gun-related initiatives before the Texas legislature.

The craft of the wise. Jan Phillips *Ms.* 3:78–79 Ja/F '93

The fanaticism that contributed to the Salem witch trials remains a force today. In 1692, 15 women and 5 men were executed for witchcraft in the New England communities of Salem and Danvers, 1 man was tortured to death, and hundreds were imprisoned. Most historians attribute the witch hunt to Puritan repression, religious intolerance, village land disputes, and rigid ideas about appropriate behavior for women. The Puritans defined witches as servants of Satan, but the people who practice witchcraft today insist that the Devil plays no part in their beliefs and practices. They follow the traditions of a pre-Christian, Goddess-centered religion called Wicca that emphasizes the unity of the sacred and secular realms. An estimated 200,000 people in the U.S. practice the Old Religion, and the Institute for the Study of American Religion asserts that witchcraft and paganism are the fastest growing religions in the country.

Their man in Waco. *The Nation* 256:505 Ap 19 '93

The National Rifle Association (NRA) has remained surprisingly silent on the Waco, Texas, siege of the Branch Davidians, given that Branch Davidian leader David Koresh symbolizes all the values for which the NRA stands. He has exercised his right to bear arms, through automatic weapons and perimeter defense, to defend himself, his home, his family, his business, and his practice of religious freedom against government interference. In Texas, Koresh was able to buy all the weaponry he wanted, so naturally when the government raided his compound, he used those weapons to shoot back, qualifying as a true NRA gun nut.

The fiery furnace. Daniel Schorr *The New Leader* 76:4 My 3 '93

The mistakes that were made in the handling of David Koresh's Branch Davidian cult in Waco, Texas, are glaring. The history of religious fanaticism and the memory of the mass suicide at Jonestown in 1978 should have taught U.S. law enforcement about the potential for self-destruction among zealots under pressure. All signs predicted the fiery conclusion to the standoff, but these signs were not recognized by the FBI's behavioral scientists, who thought that they had Koresh figured out. The hostage rescue team upon whose judgment Attorney General Janet Reno relied did not consult cult experts. Unaware of the manifestations of cult mentality, the FBI treated Koresh as if he were a rational, if criminal, person holding other people against their will, instead of a psychotic millennialist who could not be depended upon to ensure his own survival.

A brief history of the end of time. Paul S. Boyer *The New Republic* 208:30–3 My 17 '93

Cult leader David Koresh's apocalyptic beliefs have deep roots in American history. Although few of those preachers who sound eschatological themes call themselves God or stockpile AK-47s, the general contours of Koresh's beliefs are neither unique nor particularly unusual. Many Americans share Koresh's intense interest in the apocalyptic Scriptures; churches stressing apocalyptic themes are the ones experiencing the greatest growth, and prophecy paperbacks are among the highest-selling books in the country. Last-days speculation has a rich history in America, going back to the New England Puritans. Koresh's creation of a cult—and the public reaction to it—also have historical antecedents. Many of today's most respected denominations, such as the Mormons, were once denounced in the same language now directed at Koresh.

Thy kingdom come. *Newsweek* 121:52–8+ Mr 15 '93

A special section examines the government raid against the cult known as the Branch Davidians in Waco, Texas. The federal Bureau of Alcohol, Tobacco and Firearms (ATF) launched an operation against the Branch Davidians based on intelligence that the cult was amassing heavy armaments. Recently, an undercover agent who had infiltrated the cult reported an all clear to his waiting colleagues. The ATF entered into an ambush; when the shooting stopped, 4 ATF agents were dead, 15 others were wounded, and cult leader David Koresh was holed up inside the cult's compound with more than 100 followers. Criticisms about the ATF's tactics are discussed. Articles discuss Koresh's rise to power in the Branch Davidian cult, elements of a cult and several cults in the United States, and why people join cults.

Scientologists report assets of $400 million. Robert D. Hershey, Jr. *New York Times* p A 12 O 22 '93

The Church of Scientology, which recently won a decades-long drive for Federal tax exemption, has assets of about $400 million and appears to take in almost $300 million a year from counseling fees, book sales, investments, and other sources, according to documents filed with the Internal Revenue Service. The financial disclosures are in documents that the organization was required to file with the IRS in applying for tax-exempt status.

Saving kids from Satan's books. Nat Hentoff *The Progressive* 55:14–15 My '91

Attempts to control what children read have been increasing across the United States, according to an analysis by People for the American Way, which cites 244 incidents of attempted censorship in 39 states. Parents on the political and Religious Right who object to certain books on their children's mandated or optional reading lists genuinely fear that forces beyond their control have taken over the majority culture, and they believe that it is their duty to protect children from the infectious permissiveness of the larger society. Across the country, parents have objected to the language used in such books as Catcher in the Rye and My Friend Flicka, and many fundamentalist Christians are preoccupied with satanism in children's books. The censors sometimes succeed in taking books off shelves, but schools with clearly worded and structured review procedures often withstand the attacks.

As millions cheer. *The Progressive* 57:8–9 Je '93

After the tragic deaths of at least 70 cult members in the Branch Davidian compound near Waco, Texas, national public-opinion polls began reporting that an overwhelming majority of Americans found no fault with the way that law-enforcement authorities had brought the standoff to a head. When the FBI used tanks to smash through the compound walls and lob in tear gas canisters, it was still not clear how the confrontation with the cult led by David Koresh had begun on February 28. Credible answers to deeply troubling questions may be a long time coming, if they come at all. Most disturbing is the willingness of Americans to rush to the government's support before the answers are in, even in the face of overwhelming evidence that wretched mistakes were made. Democracy is in peril when millions of American citizens are ready to give that sort of blank check to police authorities.

Satanic cult survivor stories. Jeffrey S. Victor *Skeptical Inquirer* 15:274-80 Spring '91

Many psychotherapists who specialize in multiple personality disorder (MPD) credulously accept and promote the belief that satanic cults are ritually abusing children and conspiring to take over the world. These therapists base their beliefs primarily on the testimonials of MPD patients who claim to be satanic cult survivors. Such stories are usually compelling, internally consistent, and consistent with similar accounts provided by other patients, but they are not corroborated by any external evidence. Nevertheless, highly educated professionals come to accept the stories through a group conformity process that operates throughout the psychiatric communication network. Presentations and audience reactions at Culture, Cults, and Psychotherapy: Exploring Satanic and Other Cult Behavior, a psychiatric seminar sponsored by the Harding Hospital in Worthington, Ohio, are discussed.

The Satanic cult scare. David G. Bromley *Society* 28:55–66 My/Je '91

A countersubversive campaign against alleged satanism reflects an effort to give human shape to the sense of danger and vulnerability that people feel as a result of the tension over family and economy. This satanism is believed plausible despite the virtual absence of any validating physical

evidence. The satanism scare postulates the existence of a highly organized underground national network of Satanists who practice rites
geared to the exploitation and ritual sacrifice of children. Seen as the
embodiment of ultimate evil, Satanists are thought to exploit the trust
placed in them as surrogate parents by abusing children for power, plea-
sure, and profit. Assertions of tens of thousands of ritual sacrifice victims
annually are not credible, however, and reports by alleged survivors of
ritual abuse contain fantastic elements. Nevertheless, the satanism scare
has occasionally approached panic levels during the past decade.

Satanism: the scary truth. Elizabeth Karlsberg *'Teen* 37:24+ Je
'93

There are no hard figures available, but it appears Satanism is a threat in
the U.S. Law enforcement officials have become concerned about violent
and bizarre crimes that indicate signs of Satanism, the perversion of religion. Teenagers who are attracted to Satanism tend to feel cut off from
positive social influences and perhaps have experienced abuse or neglect
at home. There is also a high rate of drug and alcohol use among these
teens. The executive director of the Cult Awareness Network (CAN),
Cynthia Kisser, suggests Satanism is appealing because it "appears to offer
easy answers to complex problems." If Satanism is just another way teens
choose to be destructive, the problem lies at the source of the behavior,
not the symptom. The address for CAN, the only national, non-profit
group in the U.S. for victims of cults, is provided.

**The enemy within: why David Koresh is to blame for the tragedy at
Mount Carmel.** Gary Cartwright *Texas Monthly* 21:139+ Je '93

A blundered raid by federal agents and a botched finale do not change
the essential fact that Branch Davidian leader David Koresh is to blame
for the standoff in Waco. For 9 years, Koresh, a con man and a pathological liar, drilled his followers to prepare for Armageddon, an ending upon
which he had staked his reputation. He used classic mind-control techniques to create a crisis mentality within the compound, constantly
preaching that the end of the world was coming and that his followers
should prepare themselves. In August 1989, he announced that all earthly marriages were annulled and that all the women in the world belonged
to him. Koresh greatly reinforced his control by dissolving all sexual
unions except his own. From the moment that federal agents launched
their frontal assault on the Branch Davidian compound on the morning
of February 28, Koresh knew this was the final battle.

No sympathy for the devil. Richard N. Ostling *Time* 135:55–6 Mr
18 '90

In a recent sermon, New York's Cardinal John O'Connor stressed the
reality of evil by reading passages from The Exorcist and revealing that

priests in his archdiocese had been authorized to perform two exorcisms in the past year. O'Connor also warned that diabolically instigated violence is on the rise and that heavy-metal rock music helps spur teenagers toward satanism. While Roman Catholic theologians have largely come to view belief in demons as a naive medieval holdover, the Vatican has held fast to belief in Satan. The official Roman Ritual still includes a rite of exorcism, and the code of canon law includes rules for exorcism. In a 1986 sermon, Pope John Paul insisted on the reality of a personal devil and acknowledged the possibility of demonic possession.